DOMINOES—
67
Games & Tricks

DOMINOES—
67
Games & Tricks
by Malcolm A. Bryant

TAB BOOKS Inc.
BLUE RIDGE SUMMIT, PA. 17214

FIRST EDITION

FIRST PRINTING

Copyright © 1982 by TAB BOOKS Inc.

Printed in the United States of America

Reproduction or publication of the content in any manner, without express permission of the publisher, is prohibited. No liability is assumed with respect to the use of the information herein.

Library of Congress Cataloging in Publication Data

Bryant, Malcolm A.
    Dominoes—67 games and tricks.

    Includes index.
    1. Dominoes.   I. Title.
GV1467.B79   795.3   81-18250
ISBN 0-8306-1308-0 (pbk.)   AACR2

Acknowledgment

I would like to acknowledge the assistance of all my close friends who have helped make this book possible.

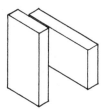

Contents

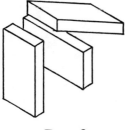

Preface

We have all played dominoes, at one time or another, by standing the blocks in a line to be toppled over with one hit. One night, I decided to investigate some of the basic tricks that can be done with a 55-piece set of dominoes.

This book represents many hours of extensive experimenting with dominoes. That does not mean this book includes all of the possible tricks that can be done with dominoes. The purpose of this book is to introduce you to the basic movements of dominoes, and then to challenge you with tricks of gradually increasing complexity.

Domino tricks can be exciting and rewarding. As they become more complex, the probability of success becomes less and less. For this reason, they form an ideal kind of solitary game where the skills and knowledge of the player are matched against the low probability of success of the trick.

As you progress and begin to master the "expert" tricks, you will no doubt be inspired to discover tricks on your own. There are countless tricks yet to be discovered. Your only limitations are the number of dominoes you have and the height of your imagination.

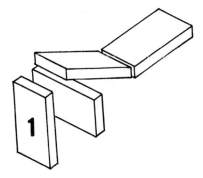

Introduction

The objective of this book is to stimulate interest in using domino tricks as a form of amusement. By domino trick, I mean an arrangement consisting of only dominoes in such a way that when they fall they will produce an amusing result. I have not included any trick requiring the building of any special apparatus. The average person can, with minimum effort, sit down at a table or other flat, smooth surface and try the tricks.

All the tricks in this book can be done with one double-nine set of dominoes. The set would contain 55 dominoes. It is strongly recommended that if you decide to increase your number of dominoes, you use only one brand. All manufacturers vary their dominoes a little in size and in the proportions of the length, to width, and depth.

Figure 1-1 shows one domino and defines its three dimensions. An *H* is always the length, *W* is always the width, and *D* refers to the depth. This holds true even if the domino is laid down. The length of one domino is referred to as the height, the width will be equal to about one-half the height, and the depth will always be the smallest dimension shown. Each domino also has three *faces* or surfaces. *Surface A* is defined as the ends, *surface B* is the front or back, and *surface C* is always the sides. Therefore, the domino shown in Fig. 1-1 is standing on its end.

Figure 1-2 shows a simple string of dominoes. Please note that each domino has a number on it. These numbers refer to when each

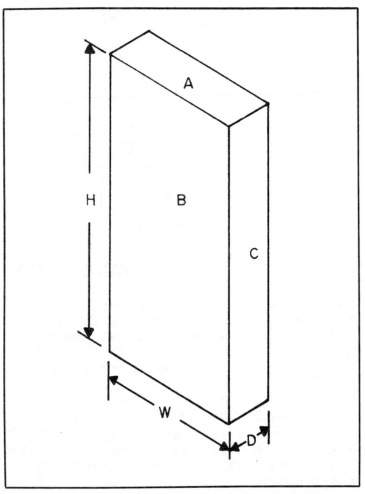

Fig. 1-1. The dimensions and forces of a single domino.

domino will fall or convey the active power in some way. In this case, domino 1 will fall over to hit domino 2, and domino 2 will then fall to hit domino 3, and so on.

In all the tricks that follow, this numbering system will be most helpful in understanding what is going on in the trick. Notice also that the power flow of the string is going from left to right. This will be the case in all but a few tricks. This direction will then be defined as *forward;* right to left will be known as *backward.* A group of dominoes that are put together to produce a trick is defined as a *system.*

Figure 1-3 shows a string of dominoes that are spaced close together. Here, you will see that domino 1 will only have to fall a short distance before hitting domino 2. This will remain true for each domino, in turn, as they fall over. This close spacing will give a fast-forward movement.

Figure 1-4 shows an increased spacing between all the dominoes. In this case, it will take longer for domino 1 to fall and hit domino 2. This would remain true throughout the system so as to give a slow-forward movement. You can use the spacing to determine the speed you want to get from "here to there" in a trick.

In this book, I very seldom give a measurement in inches or feet because each domino set varies. What might work for one set of dominoes will not work for another. For this reason, use the dimensions given in Fig. 1-1 as units to help in the placement of the dominoes. This allows the advantage of using 1 domino as a unit of measure. Figure 1-5 shows how to measure a distance of one W with a domino. Figure 1-6 is an example of measuring a distance of H to D.

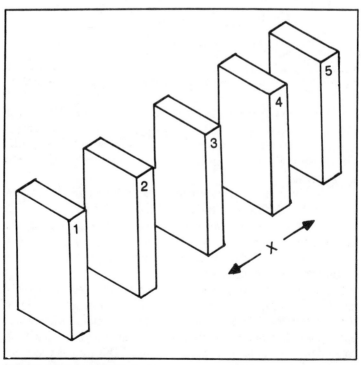

Fig. 1-2. A simple string of dominoes.

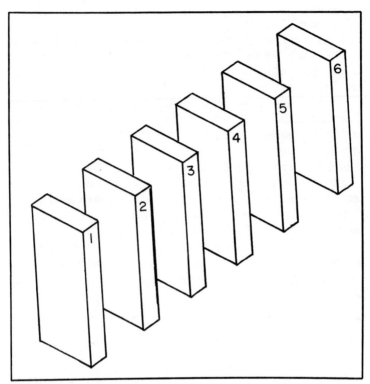

Fig. 1-3. A string of closely spaced dominoes will give a fast-forward motion.

In Figure 1-7, domino 1 is falling over to hit domino 2. Note that Fig. 1-7 gives two views of this. Figure 1-7A is the normal three-dimensional view and 1-7B is a front view. Any of three views can be given along with a three-dimensional view to help make a point or to show a result.

Note what I call a *movement arrow* in Fig. 1-78. This arrow shows the path that this domino will follow as it falls.

Figure 1-8 shows domino 1 falling against domino 2 that has been rotated by 90 degrees. Note that domino 2 cannot fall over so it slides in a forward direction. This shows the importance of the arrangement of one domino to another.

Figure 1-9 shows another arrangement between dominoes 1 and 2. Domino 2 is offset from domino 1 as is shown in the top view of Fig. 1-9 B. With the dominoes so arranged, domino 1 will only hit about one-fourth of domino 2's face. In so doing, domino 2 will be rotated before it falls to the playing surface. This happens because the surface friction holds half of domino 2's end in place when the

4

friction of the other half has been overpowered by the force from domino 1. The changing of the placement of the two dominoes gives a whole new result. Each placement of any number of dominoes will have a unique output.

Figure 1-10 shows a system consisting of three dominoes. As they are set up, the dominoes will fall as shown by the arrow in Fig. 1-11. Domino 1 hits domino 2 which falls forward. Domino 3 will then lose its support and fall backward. With this in mind, note Fig. 1-12 where there is a new system that contains five dominoes. As this system falls, the dominoes will also fall backward (as in Fig. 1-11). Figure 1-13 shows how the dominoes will fall.

Look at Fig. 1-14. This is the same system as shown in Fig. 1-12, but the spacing is reduced between the dominoes. When this system falls, you get a whole new result (as shown in Fig. 1-15).

All of the dominoes will fall in a forward direction. Not only is the arrangement of the dominoes important, but spacing between

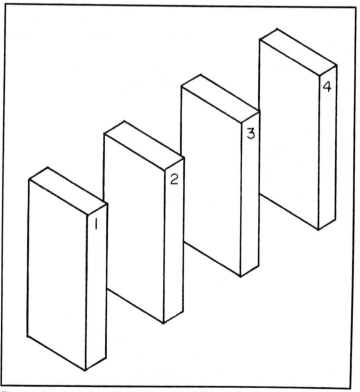

Fig. 1-4. A string with wide spacing will have a slow-forward motion.

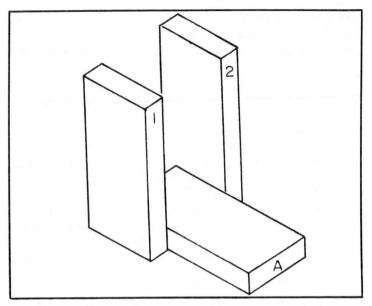

Fig. 1-5. Using a domino as a ruler. Here the distance between dominoes one and two is equal to one W.

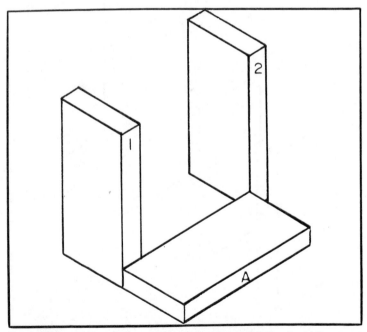

Fig. 1-6. Measuring a distance of H to D between dominoes 1 and 2.

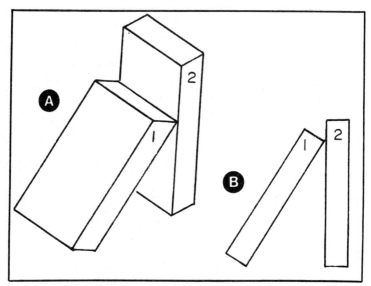

Fig. 1-7. The falling of a single domino (domino 2) is caused by the surface "holding" its base as a forward force is applied by the previous domino (1).

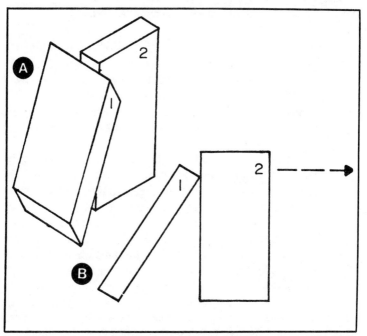

Fig. 1-8. Turning the domino (2) 90 degrees will reinforce it so that is will not fall, but it will slide across the surface. Note the movement arrow.

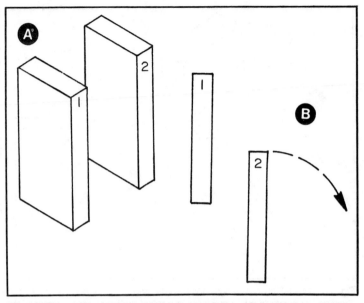

Fig. 1-9. The relationship between the dominoes (1 and 2) is such that one corner of domino 2 moves forward as the other is held fast by the table. This results in the domino turning before it falls. Note the movement arrow.

the dominoes can have an important effect on what the system will do. In Fig. 1-12, note that there are two dominoes marked A and B. These dominoes are so marked because they are not hit by any of the power-carrying dominoes. This does not mean they will not fall. What it shows is that they are used for some other purpose in the system. In the case of domino A, it is used as a support to hold domino 2 off the table.

Non-active dominoes (those that do not have a number) can be used as supports to go under other dominoes and as reinforcement to keep another domino from moving. Figure 1-16 shows two means of simplifying a complex system of dominoes. You will not see much use of them until latter chapters, but they are given here for your reference. Figure 1-16(A) is used when one domino has been removed from the system to help show the complete picture. Note that it's former location is shown by the use of a dashed square.

In some systems, you will have to remove a larger part of the system. Removal dominoes are shown in a dotted square. A large arrow shows how to move the dominoes back into the system. When this means of simplifying is used, a drawing of the completed system will also be given to show where these dominoes are placed.

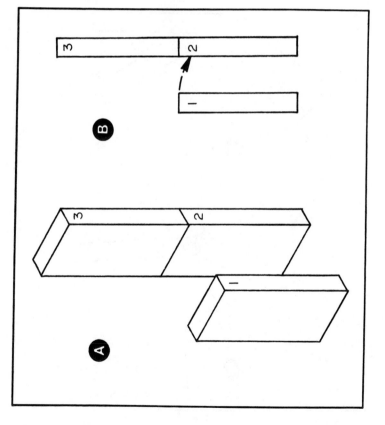

Fig. 1-10. As force is applied to domino 1, it falls and hits domino 2. Figure 1-11 shows the results.

9

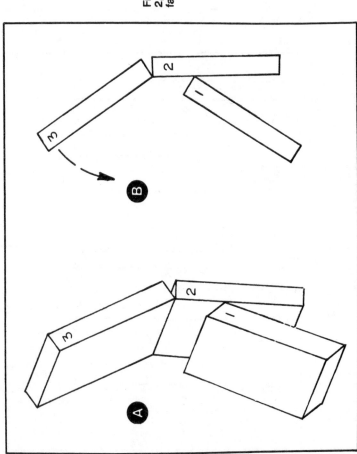

Fig. 1-11. As domino 1 hits domino 2, domino 3 loses its support and falls in the direction shown.

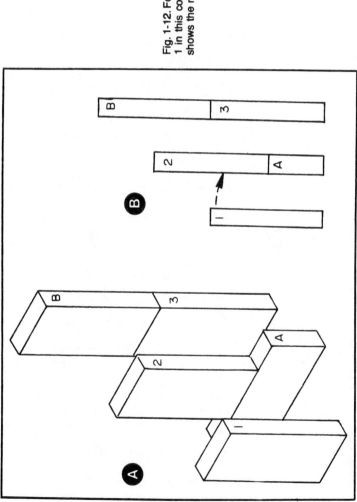

Fig. 1-12. Force is applied to domino 1 in this configuration. Figure 1-13 shows the results.

11

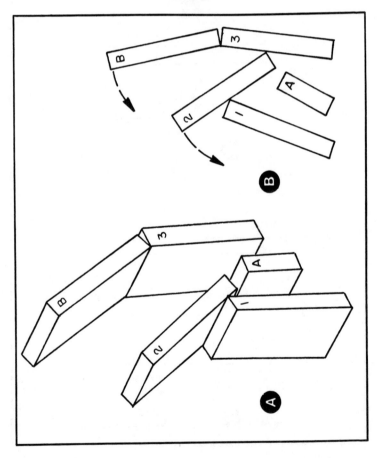

Fig. 1-13. Domino 1 hits domino 2, which hits domino 3. The assembly then collapses upon itself.

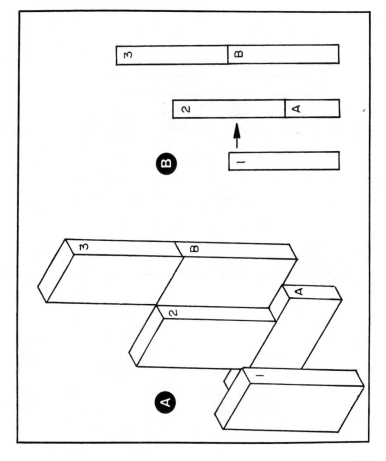

Fig. 1-14. This assembly looks like the one in Fig. 1-12 except that the spacing between the dominoes has been reduced. Force is applied to domino 1.

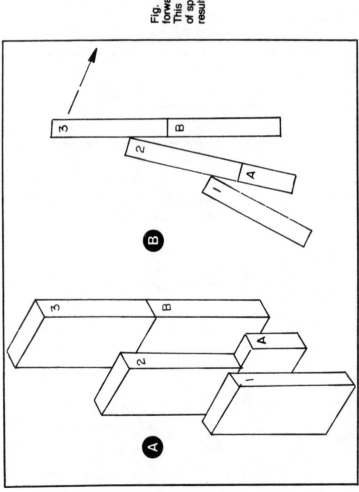

Fig. 1-15. All five dominoes fall forward. Note the movement arrow. This demonstrates the importance of spacing in achieving the desired results.

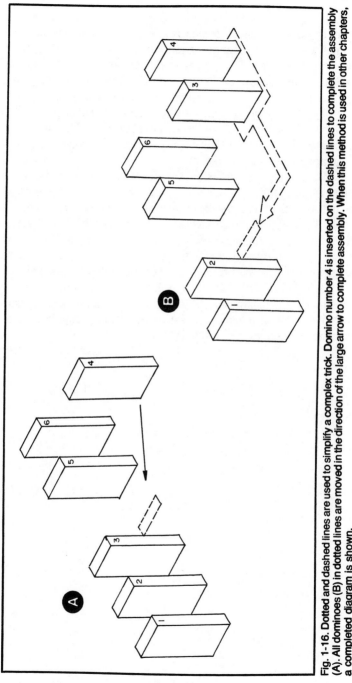

Fig. 1-16. Dotted and dashed lines are used to simplify a complex trick. Domino number 4 is inserted on the dashed lines to complete the assembly (A). All dominoes (B) in dotted lines are moved in the direction of the large arrow to complete assembly. When this method is used in other chapters, a completed diagram is shown.

Each trick is given two ratings right after the name of the trick. The first rating is called *complexity* and it gives a rough idea of how complex the trick is. The rating range is from 1 to 5. A rating of 1 is for very simple; and 5 is for very hard. The other rating is for the *probability of success* (or POS for short). This is used to give a general idea as to how often the trick will work. This rating range is from 1 to 5. A rating of 1 means it will probably never work and 5 means that it will work about 95 percent of the time. The ratings are arbitrary. They should only be used as a very rough means of comparing one trick to another.

As you go through this book, you will notice that some of the more complicated tricks have a very low POS rating. These tricks do not stand much of a chance of working. Why are they used in this book? They are a challenge to the more dedicated domino trickster. As in any game of solitaire, the fun is derived from knowing that you have beaten the odds by completing the trick. For this reason a wide selection of POS-rated tricks have been included in this book.

Before you try the tricks, remember that this book does not contain, by any means, all of the possible tricks that can be done with dominoes. This book should stimulate your imagination so that you can develop your own domino tricks.

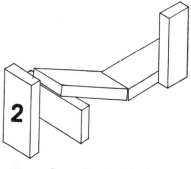

Beginning Tricks

This chapter describes how to get the first domino of the string to fall over. This could easily be done by the touch of your finger; but that would be to simple! Why not put some excitement and ingenuity to work for you in getting your tricks started? There is nothing like *scoring a goal* or using a *standing launcher* to get your show off to a good start.

All of these starting tricks do not have the same operating principles. All tricks have their own characteristics which will allow you to choose the kind of trick that suits you or your table. NOTE: As with any trick, the aim of the shooter is all important for the trick to work. Tricks are rated with the assumption that the *flicked domino* or *slide domino* is placed close enough to the target so as to achieve a hit every time.

SIMPLE SLIDE START

Complexity: 1
POS: 5

With this trick (Fig. 2-1), domino 1 is flicked with your forefinger across the table to hit the base of domino 2. Domino 2 then transmits its power to the upper half of domino 3. Domino 3 is thereby toppled to hit domino 4 and thus continues the string.

When you set up this trick, make sure dominoes 2 and A are against domino 3. This gives maximum power to domino 3 to continue the string. Domino 1 can be flicked from any distance as long as you are a good shot and hit domino 2.

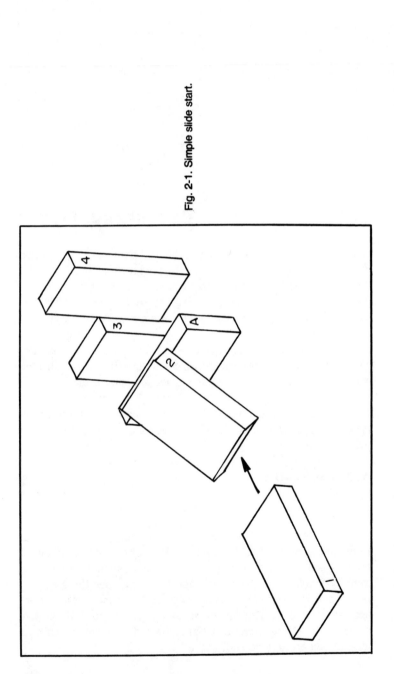

Fig. 2-1. Simple slide start.

SIMPLE FLYING START

Complexity: 1
POS: 4

This trick (Fig. 2-2) has a spectacular flying start. Domino 1 is flicked through the air to hit domino 2. Domino 1 sits on domino A as shown in Figs. 2-3 and 2-4. Figure 2-3 shows the angle for a low-flying domino. Figure 2-4 shows the angle for a high-flying trajectory.

SIMPLE RECOVERY WALL

Complexity: 1
POS: 5

With the preceding trick, the distance that you can shoot domino 1 from is severely limited by the aim of the shooter. It would be far more exciting to be able to move this domino back several more feet from its target and still keep the trick's POS high. The

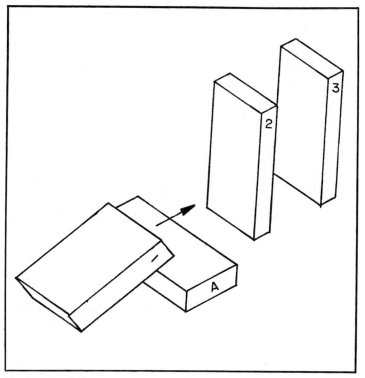

Fig. 2-2. Simple flying start.

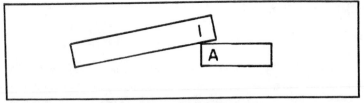

Fig. 2-3. The simple flying start for a low-flying trajectory.

simple recovery wall shown in Fig. 2-5 does just that by being used in place of domino 2 in the simple flying start of Fig. 2-2.

As shown in Fig. 2-5, the service area of the target has been increased by four. If any one of the dominoes numbered 1 is hit by the flying domino, it will topple over to hit its corresponding domino number 2. This process will continue with domino 2 hitting domino 3 and then domino 3 hitting domino 4. Domino 4 can be used to continue the string to the next trick. If any combination of domino 1's are hit by the flying domino, the string will continue.

All the lines of dominoes are spaced by a distance of about one domino. This is done to increase the instability of the system. It will be more sensitive to any hitting domino.

ECONOMY RECOVERY WALL

Complexity: 1
POS: 4

Here is another version of the simple recovery wall. Please note that Fig. 2-6 is a rear view of the system; this view shows how all the dominoes are related. Remember (from Chapter 1) that dashed lines in front of domino 3 are used to show where domino 4 is placed. This system falls exactly like the simple recovery wall.

One point of difference is that the economy wall uses one less domino then the simple wall—hence its name economy. But everything is a balance of factors. In this case, you save one domino,

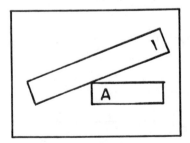

Fig. 2-4. The simple flying start set up for a high-flying trajectory.

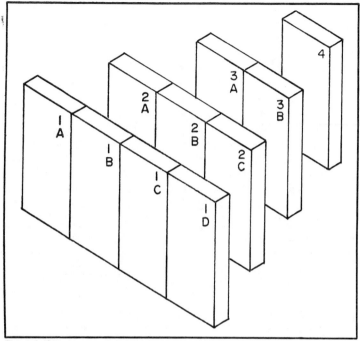

Fig. 2-5. Simple recovery wall.

but your POS is decreased from 5 to 4. The system is less dependable.

DEPENDABLE FLYING START

Complexity: 1
POS: 5

Another way of increasing the distance between the *target* and the shooter is to use the target as shown in Fig. 2-7. To understand why this will allow you to increase the spacing, you first have to understand the drawbacks of the simple flying start (Fig. 2-2). With this trick, you have to hit domino number 2 above its center of gravity or with sufficient force to make it fall to hit domino 3.

If you increase the distance between target and shooter, the trick becomes increasingly harder to accomplish. For example, it is entirely possible for the shooter to give domino 1 sufficient power to fly through the air and hit domino 2 at its base. This would result in domino 2 falling toward the shooter and not hitting domino 3 as intended.

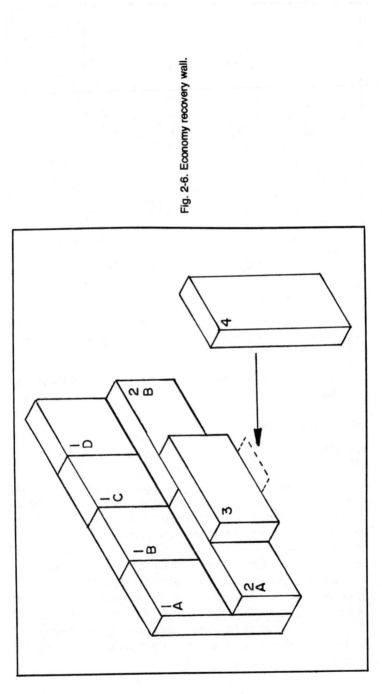

Fig. 2-6. Economy recovery wall.

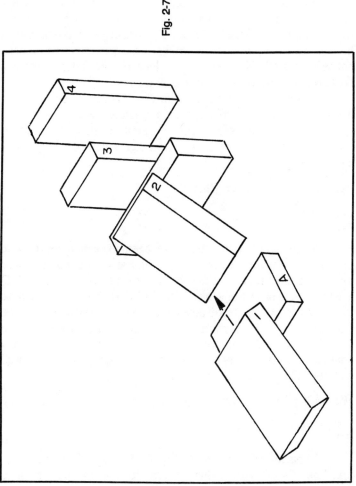

Fig. 2-7. Dependable flying start.

To prevent this possibility from happening, combine the target of the simple slide start (Fig. 2-1) with the idea of the flying domino (Fig. 2-2). Note the combination shown in Fig. 2-7. If domino 1 hits the base of domino 2, its power would still be transmitted to the top of domino 3 to continue the string. The service area of the target is increased. You can increase the shooting distance as you prefer.

THE STACKED START

Complexity: 2
POS: 4

Here is the simple slide start with a little added challenge. As shown in Fig. 2-8, a stack of dominoes (A B and two dominoes between dominoes 1 and 3) have been added. The idea behind this trick is to hit domino 2 with domino 1 with sufficient force to make it hit domino 3 and continue the string. At the same time, there must not be too much force so that domino 1 will remain under the stack of domino A and B (as shown in Fig. 2-9).

The possibility of continuing the string is very likely (POS: 4), but the probability of domino 1 remaining under dominoes A and B is very remote. This trick gives the satisfaction of starting the string, and at the same time it offers the possibility of accomplishing a very unlikely event.

DEPENDABLE RECOVERY WALL

Complexity: 2
POS: 5

To this point, two ways have been explained for how to increase the distance between the target and the shooter. These methods are by increasing the service area of the target (Fig. 2-5) and by the use of a domino on a slant (Fig. 2-7). Now combine these two ideas to get the most dependable recovery wall that can be made. In Fig. 2-10, the system contains both an increased service area and slanted dominoes. Any sliding dominoes or flying dominoes that hit any one or combination of dominoes of the wall will very likely continue the string.

THE BACKWARD FALLING START

Complexity: 3
POS: 3

The backward falling start (Fig. 2-11) is a trick that uses the principles discussed up to this point, but it has a new twist. Domino

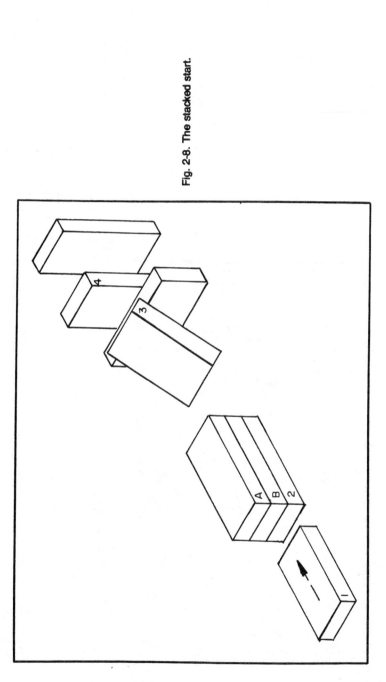

Fig. 2-8. The stacked start.

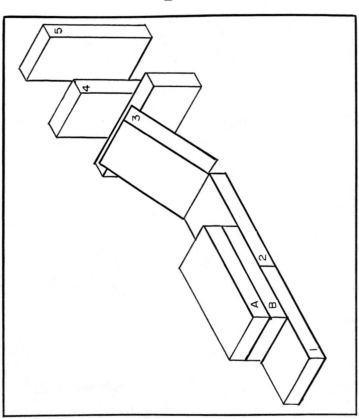

Fig. 2-9. The stacked start in progress.

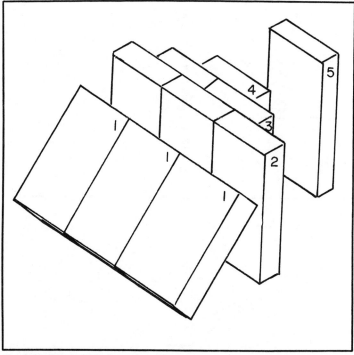

Fig. 2-10. Dependable recovery wall.

1 is slid to hit domino 2 with an added amount of force. Domino 2 then transmits this power to the base of domino 3. Domino 3 then falls toward the shooter. This is backward from how it would normally have fallen. As domino 3 falls backward, its base hits domino 4's base and makes it fall backward. As domino 4 falls, its base hits domino 5 on its base. This power is then continued up domino 6 to the top of domino 7. Domino 7 then falls forward to continue the string. Figure 2-12 shows the progressive motion of all the dominoes in the trick.

SIMPLE DOMINO LAUNCHER

Complexity: 2
POS: 3

With this flying start trick, domino 1 is placed on domino A so that it's center line is at A's edge (as shown in Fig. 2-13). Domino 2 is then placed on domino 1 so that its center line is on domino 1's edge. With this arrangement, applying downward power to domino

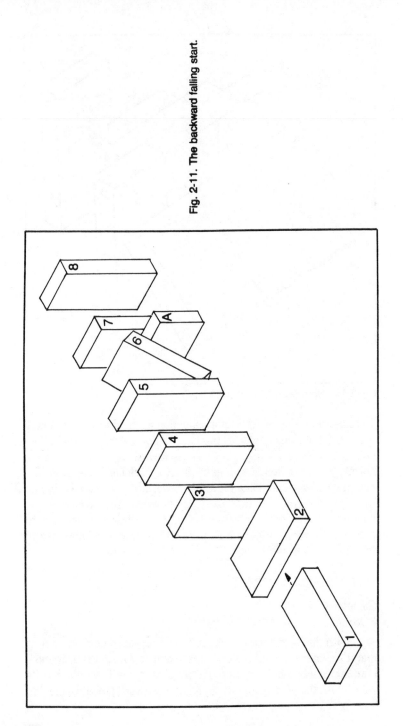

Fig. 2-11. The backward falling start.

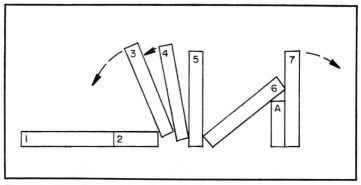

Fig. 2-12. The backward flying start in progress.

1 will cause domino 2 to fly up. This kind of launcher sends the domino into a very high trajectory with a short forward distance. Like all flicking tricks, this one might require a little practice to get used to. After you are acquainted with this trick, you will be able to easily flick a domino over a wall of up to three dominoes high.

ROUNDABOUT DOMINO LAUNCHER

Complexity: 3
POS: 4

Here is another means of launching a domino over a wall or barrier (Fig. 2-14). In this system, domino 1 is set on domino A (as shown in Fig. 2-15) so that its center line (CL) is to one side of domino A. This will allow dominoes 1 and 2 to balance on top of domino A. By hitting down on domino 1, domino 2 will be launched on a low-median trajectory.

Figure 2-16 shows another variation of this same launcher. Domino 2 is placed on its side on domino 1. This would provide a higher flying trajectory.

TARGET SHOOTING

Complexity: 1
POS: 2

Target shooting (Fig. 2-17) is an alternative to the wall used with other launcher tricks. The idea is simply to use a low-flying trajectory trick to knock off domino 1 from its table of dominoes (A, B, and C). If a high-flying trajectory trick is used, the *table* can be made higher so that you are able to hit the target.

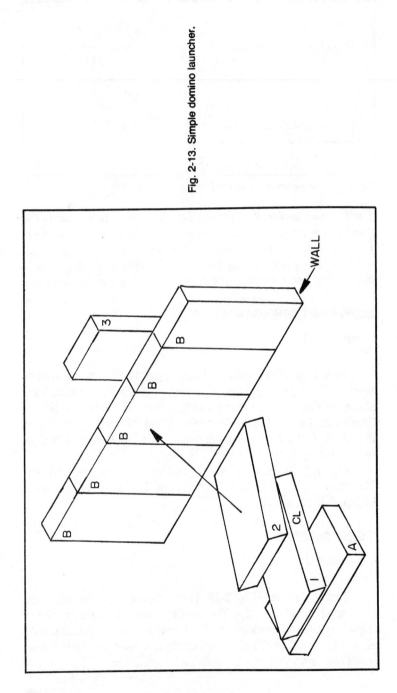

Fig. 2-13. Simple domino launcher.

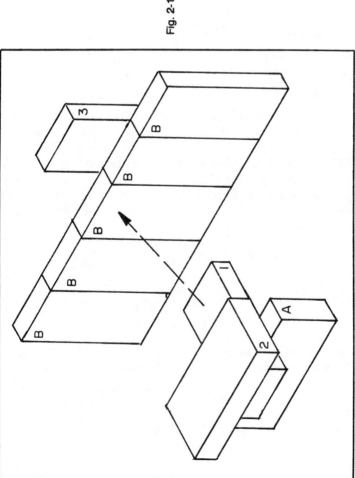

Fig. 2-14. Roundabout domino launcher.

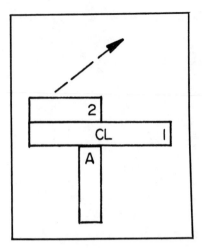

Fig. 2-15. Side view of roundabout domino launcher.

SCORING A GOAL

Complexity: 1
POS: 2

Here is another alternative to the wall or target shooting. This consists of a table of dominoes, A, B, and C of Fig. 2-18, and two dominoes (D and E) on top forming a goal post as is used in football. The idea is to hit the flying domino through domino D and domino E without knocking either of them off the table. If need be, the goal post can be made wider by using three supporting dominoes with two cross members on top. This would result in a goal opening of about 2H-2D.

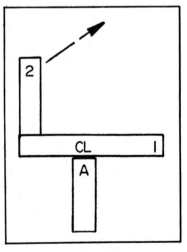

Fig. 2-16. Another variation of the roundabout launcher.

DUEL STARTER

Complexity: 2
POS: 4

This trick is simply the roundabout launcher (Fig. 2-14) with a domino added to make it a duel starter (Fig. 2-19). With one hit, the power of your finger will start the strings in opposite directions. Figure 2-20 shows how this is done. As you hit down on domino 1, domino 2B flys to hit domino 3B to continue the string. At the same

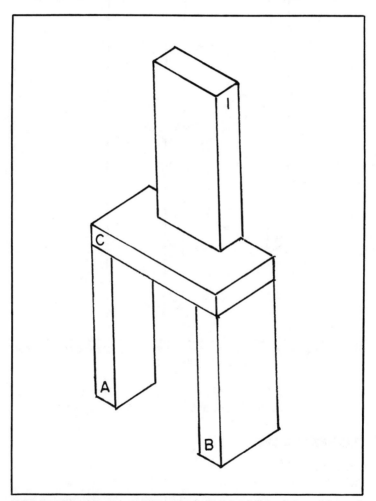

Fig. 2-17. With target shooting, the object is simply to hit domino number 1 and knock it off using a flying-start trick.

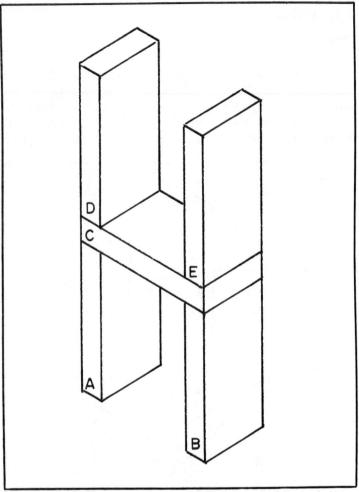

Fig. 2-18. With scoring a goal, the idea is to fly the launched domino between dominoes D and E (without knocking them down).

time—as domino 1 turns on A—it knocks over domino 2A which in turn will hit domino 3A (not shown) to continue the string.

STANDING LAUNCHER

Complexity: 2
POS: 4

The standing launcher (Fig. 2-21) gives the shooter the best control over the projectile. Domino 1 is placed on domino A with its

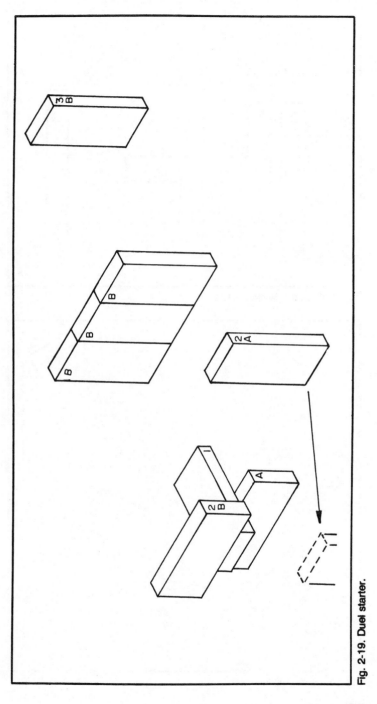

Fig. 2-19. Duel starter.

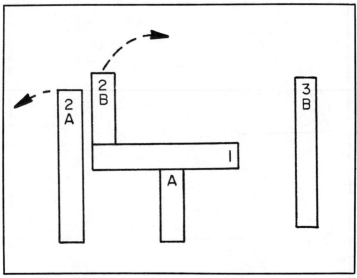

Fig. 2-20. Side view showing the motions of a duel starter.

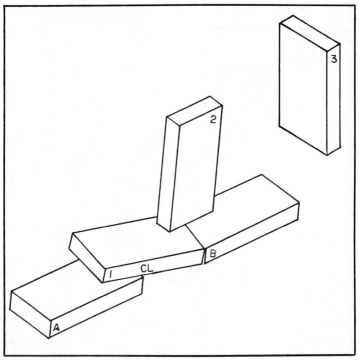

Fig. 2-21. Standing launcher.

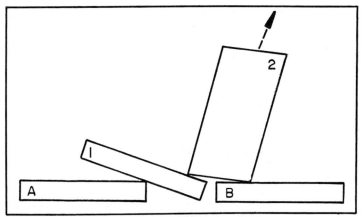

Fig. 2-22. A standing launcher set up for high trajectory.

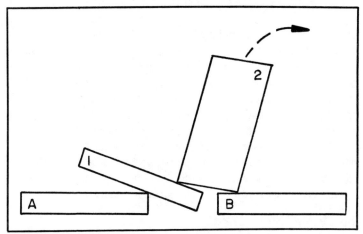

Fig. 2-23. A standing launcher set up for a low trajectory.

center line on domino A's edge. Domino B is used as support for one side of domino 2 (as shown in Fig. 2-21).

Figure 2-22 shows the placement of domino 2 on domino 1 and domino B so as to give a high-flying trajectory. Figure 2-23 shows the placement of domino 2 for a low-flying trajectory. The power output of the launcher can be adjusted somewhat by changing the location of the center line of dominoes as compaired with the edge of domino A.

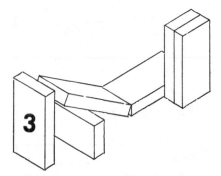

3

Simple Continuing Tricks

In this chapter, I will assume your strings of dominoes have a means of being started. The method can be as simple as a finger or as complex as one of the launcher tricks described in Chapter 2. The last falling domino of the started string will be the only power input for these continuing-trick strings. The continuing strings all provide a falling domino as an output that can be used to power one or more other continuing strings, or one or more finishing tricks (see Chapter 8). As you are trying out a trick for the first time, I strongly recommend that you use five or six *lead dominoes* to lead into the trick. This will allow the dominoes to pick up speed and power, and to give you the best chance for success.

RAISED CONTINUING STRING

Complexity: 1
POS: 5

This trick consists of simply taking the standard string shown in Chapter 1 (Fig. 1-2) and raising it by placing it on a row of supporting dominoes (Fig. 3-1). The operation is straight forward and the placement of the dominoes is not critical.

THE SQUARE ARCHES

Complexity: 2
POS: 4

With this trick (Fig. 3-2), you are transmitting the input power up through the top of the "arches" through dominoes 3, 4, and 5.

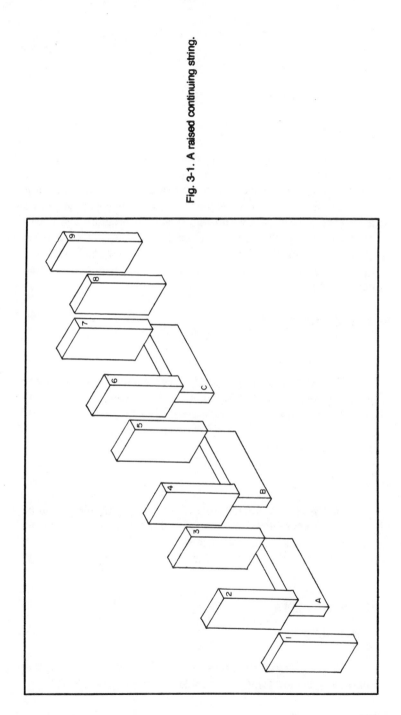

Fig. 3-1. A raised continuing string.

Domino 7 gives you the power output to continue another string. Because of the unstable nature of this system, the trick can be expanded with up to seven arches instead of the three shown.

THE FALLING BRIDGE

Complexity: 2
POS: 5

As shown in Fig. 3-3, the bridge—consisting of dominoes 3, 4, and 5—in this trick will fall as power is applied to one system. As the bridge is made longer (up to 10 dominoes instead of three) it takes on a different aspect and it will look more like a bridge. When it is longer it will also be much stronger then before and it will remain standing at the completion of the trick. As you expand the bridge, make sure all of the floor dominoes (3, 4, and 5, etc.) are tightly up against one another to give maximum power transfer from one domino to the next.

SIDE SLIDING STRING

Complexity: 1
POS: 5

This trick (Fig. 3-4) is pretty much self-explanatory. Power goes into domino 1 and out with domino 8. Dominoes 3, 4, and 5 will remain standing when the trick is completed.

PUSH ROD CONTINUATION

Complexity: 1
POS: 5

This very simple trick (Fig. 3-5) has a low profile. It can be used to go underneath another trick. Dominoes 3 and 4 remain standing after the trick is completed. This is true for up to 4 push rods (instead of the two shown) if the surface of the table is not to great.

DOWN AND UNDER

Complexity: 3
POS: 5

This is a very interesting system. It was a very low profile that makes it ideal for going under tricks or objects (Fig. 3-6).

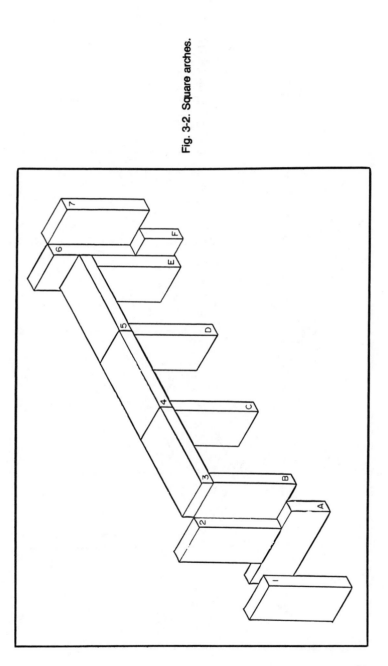

Fig. 3-2. Square arches.

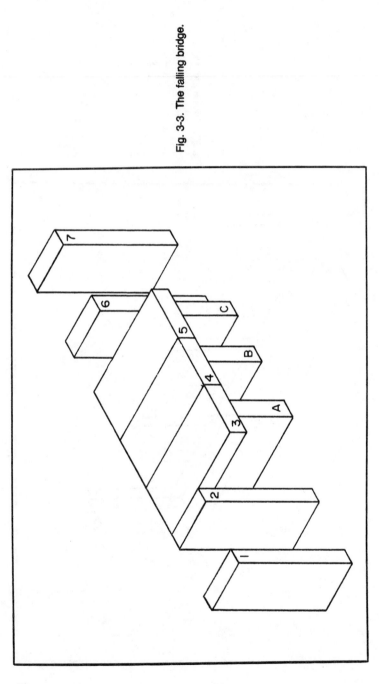

Fig. 3-3. The falling bridge.

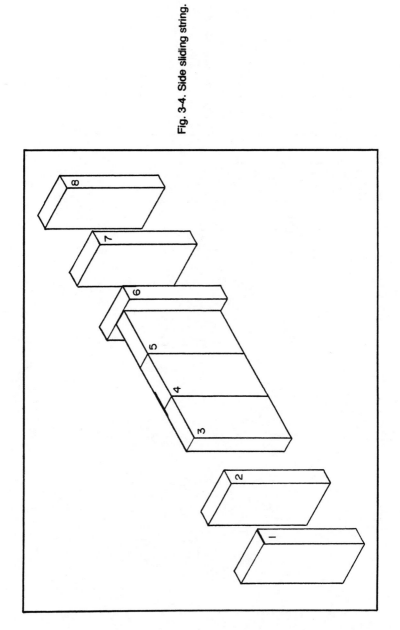

Fig. 3-4. Side sliding string.

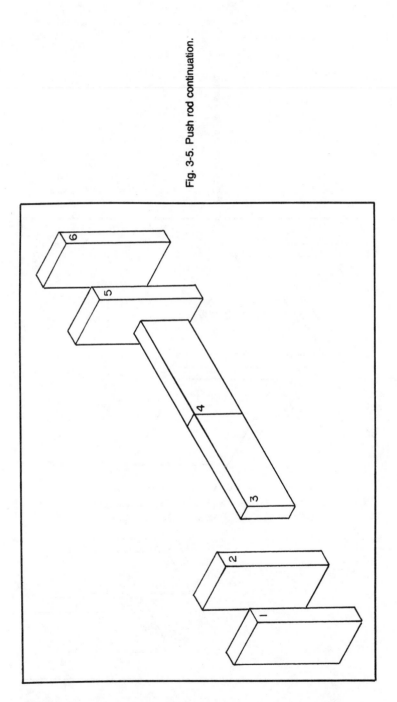

Fig. 3-5. Push rod continuation.

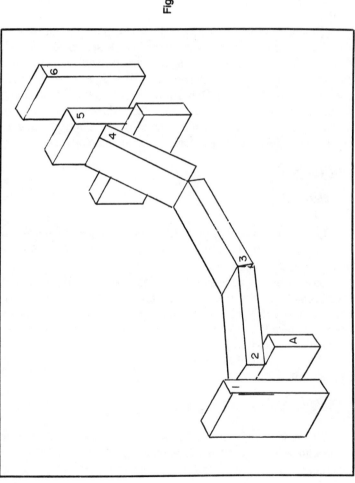

Fig. 3-6. Down and under.

Domino 2 should be placed on domino A in such a way that when domino 1 falls it will hit domino 2 on it's end. This power will go down domino 2, through domino 3 and up domino 4 to continue the string. Always make sure that domino 4 is against domino 5 to give maximum power transfer.

Another one or two dominoes can be added with domino 3 to make the trick longer, but the POS would be reduced. The amount it would be reduced would depend on the friction of the playing surface.

TOPSY-TURVY WORLD

Complexity: 3
POS: 4

This odd-looking trick (Fig. 3-7) is simply a different twist to the simple string. The string of dominoes are set up so that each domino has one end on the playing surface and one end on a supporting domino. The supporting dominoes (A, B, C, etc.) are at a spacing of about W and D between each other. The standing dominoes are then placed in the center of each supporting domino. Balancing these dominoes is not often easy, but this trick could go on just about forever—if you have the time and patience.

SIDE FALLS

Complexity: 2
POS: 4

In side falls (as in topsy-turvy world), dominoes have one end propped (Fig. 3-8). This time, rotate them 90 degrees and have them fall over on their sides.

Spacing between the supporting dominoes (A and B) should be about W and D to give maximum reliability. Also, dominoes 5 and 6 have to form a straight line to insure that they will hit each other when they fall. This trick could be expanded to four side dominoes (instead of two) without changing the POS much.

FALLING ARCHES

Complexity: 2
POS: 4

This funny-looking trick (Fig. 3-9) is included as a challenge for those who have a steady hand. Dominoes 3 and 4 and 5 and 6 are set together to form arches. Dominoes 4 and 5 touch each other at their

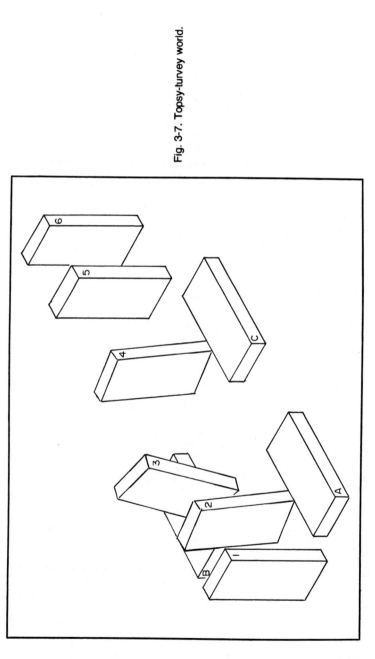

Fig. 3-7. Topsy-turvey world.

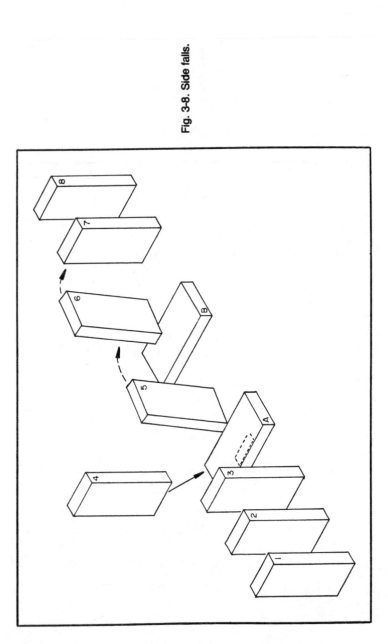

Fig. 3-8. Side falls.

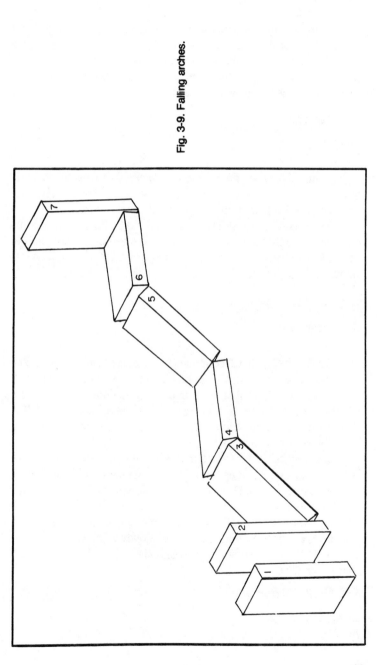

Fig. 3-9. Falling arches.

bases to give each other support. Dominoes 2 and 7 are set up before the arches to also add support (see Fig. 3-10).

The difficulty of the trick depends a lot on the friction of the playing surface that is being used. If your playing surface will not allow you to form the arches, a piece of paper can be placed on the table. The paper will give you enough friction to build. This trick works most of the time because it is so unstable that any small amount of power input will make it fall.

THE SIDE SLIDE

Complexity: 2
POS: 4

Sliding dominoes on a table is explained in Chapter 2. I will now introduce dominoes sliding upon other dominoes. The side slide (Fig. 3-11) is a simple example of this kind of trick.

Power comes into the trick and domino 2 hits domino 3 on its end. Domino 3 then slides down domino B, where it hits domino 4 to continue the string. This trick is so simple that if you set it up as it is shown in Fig. 3-11 it will work 95 percent of the time.

SLIDE AND WOBBLE

Complexity: 2
POS: 4

This trick (Fig. 3-12) combines two aspects in one system: The slide and the wobble. Domino 2 will hit domino 3, which, in turn, will slide on top of domino A, to end up pushing on domino 4. Domino 4 will wobble forward to stand upright. If it is hit too hard, it will fall to either side. As domino 4 stands up, it more than likely hits domino 5 to continue the string.

The only critical distance in this system is between domino 4 (sitting at an angle) and domino 5. This distance should not be over one because domino 4 D might then not hit domino 5. The best way to set up this trick is to balance domino 4 on domino A so that it will just stay there and not fall toward domino 5. Domino 3 can then be placed on domino A. With one hand, slowly slide it up to touch domino 4. As you are doing this, steady the rest of the system with your other hand.

THE SHORT TOWER DROP

Complexity: 3
POS: 4

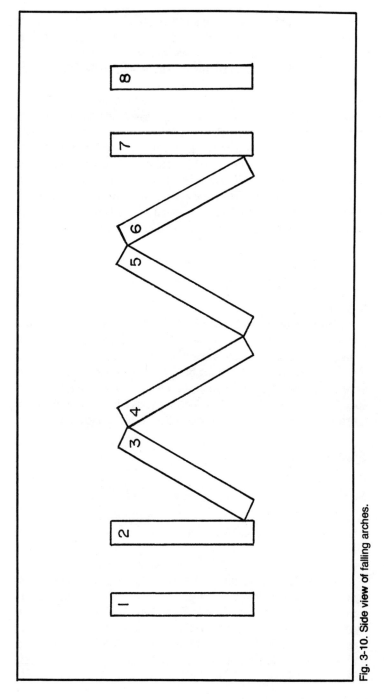

Fig. 3-10. Side view of falling arches.

Here is a short tower. It might start to look complex, but it is really very simple. The majority of the dominoes in the trick (Fig. 3-13) are used to reinforce the two moving dominoes (2 and 3). Domino 1 hits domino 2, and domino 2 slides domino 3 off the edge so that it falls to the table to hit domino 4.

The easiest way to assemble this trick is to start at the base in the center with domino A. Then you can easily add dominoes C, B, and D (D is almost hidden behind 2 and 3) to the system. Dominoes 2 and 3 are then added with one hand as you hold domino B and D with your other hand. Dominoes 2 and 3 are slid forward until domino 3 is about to fall. Dominoes E and F are added to complete the tower. Note that domino 2 will overhang a little on the front of domino C so as to give domino 3 enough room to balance. Domino 4 should not be over a distance of one W from the end of domino 3.

THE SIMPLE Y

Complexity: 1
POS: 5

Figure 3-14 shows the very simple idea of a *Y* or a *branch* in a line of dominoes. Note that there are two dominoes each labeled 3, 4, and 5. Dominoes with the same number will fall at the same time. For example, domino 2 will hit both dominoes numbered 3 at the same time, both dominoes numbered 4 will fall at the same time, and so on. In Fig. 3-14, each pair of dominoes has a letter. For example, there is a domino 3A and a domino 3B in this illustration.

DROP AND FLIP

Complexity: 3
POS: 3

The branch (Fig. 3-14) can be used to make a slightly more complex trick. In Fig. 3-15, notice that dominoes 5, 6, 7, and A are all surrounded by a line of dots with a large arrow. The dominoes will move in the direction of the arrow.

Figure 3-16 shows how much to move the group of dominoes by giving a completed picture after the move. You do not have to set up and move the group. This is done only to simplify a complex system. Imagine trying to understand Fig. 3-16 without having seen Fig. 3-15, and you will see why this is done. Look at Figs. 3-15, 3-16, and 3-17; note that dominoes 1, 2, and 3 have been left out to help reduce confusion.

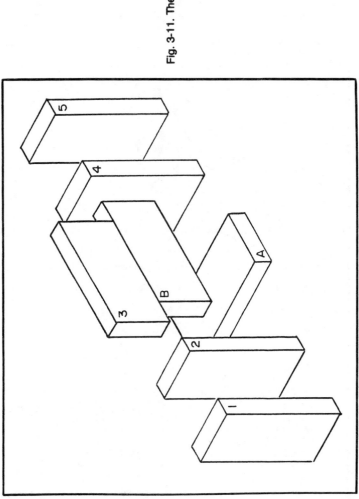

Fig. 3-11. The side slide.

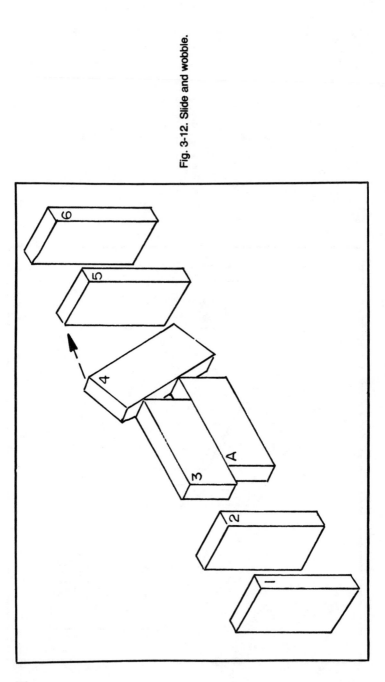

Fig. 3-12. Slide and wobble.

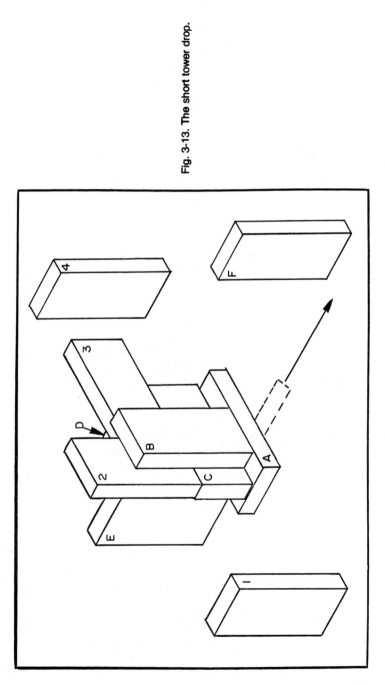

Fig. 3-13. The short tower drop.

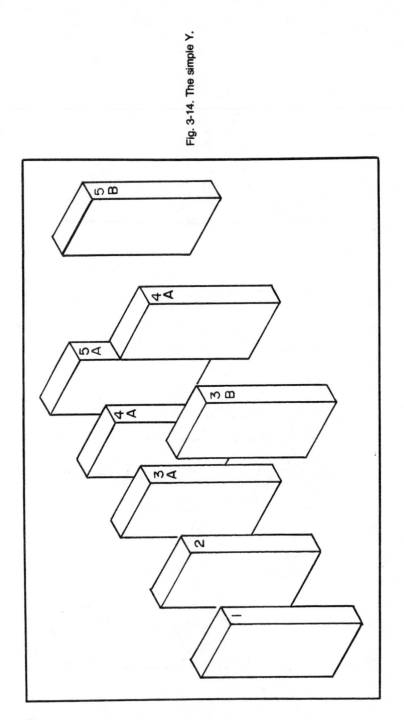

Fig. 3-14. The simple Y.

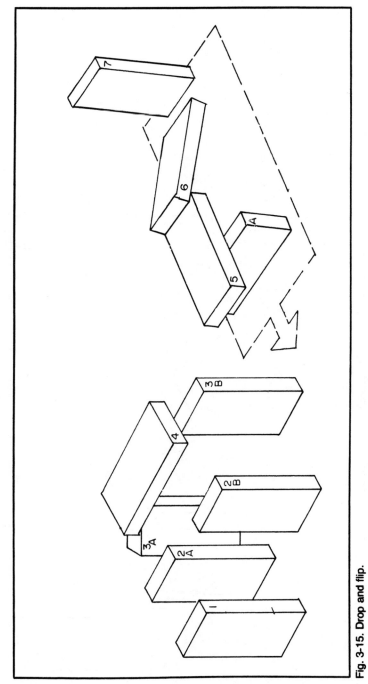

Fig. 3-15. Drop and flip.

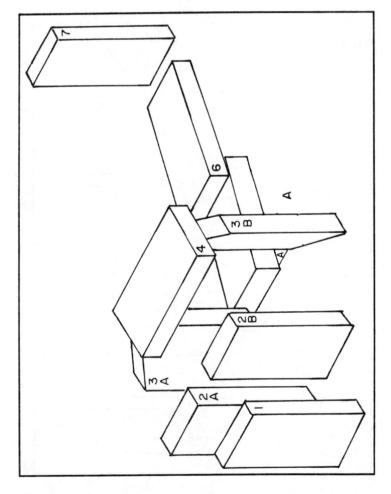

Fig. 3-16. Drop and flip completely assembled.

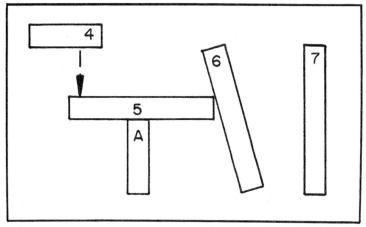

Fig. 3-17. The forces acting in the drop and flip.

As you apply power to this system, domino 1 is carried by dominoes 2A and 2B to topple dominoes 3A and 3B at the same time. As they fall, domino 4 also falls as shown by the movement arrow in Fig. 3-17. Domino 4 then hits domino 5 which is balanced on domino A at such an angle to hold domino 6. As you can guess, domino 5 is rotated and acts as a lever to throw domino 6 over its center of gravity to hit domino 7 and continue the string. Figure 3-17 shows the movement of the dominoes.

As you are setting up this trick, note the following or the trick will not work. Make sure you turn domino 3A and domino 3B outward from the system so that they do not hit domino A as they fall over. Also make sure that domino 5 is under domino 4 by a distance of one-half W so that it will hit the maximum force. Domino 6 should be on the verge of falling to an upright position. If it is laying down too low, domino 5 will not have enough power to get it over its center of gravity.

Even if you do set this system up properly, the POS is fairly low because the trick is so complex. Don't get discouraged. With a little practice, you will be able to get it working.

SEESAW

Complexity: 3
POS: 3

With the seesaw, use the same type of Y used to start the previous tricks. As you can see in Figs. 3-18 and 3-19, domino 4

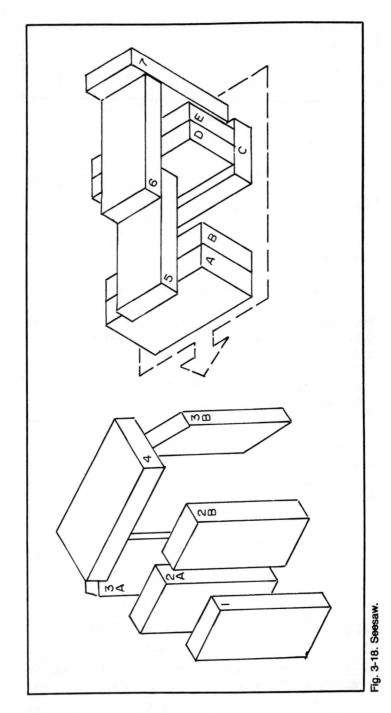

Fig. 3-18. Seesaw.

60

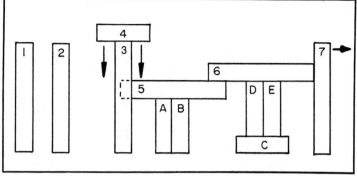

Fig. 3-19. The forces in the seesaw continuation.

drops onto domino 5 causing it to pivot on dominoes A and B. As the front end of domino 5 goes down, its rear is lifted and pivots domino 6 onto base of domino D and domino E. As 6 pivots, it hits domino 7 and transmits enough power to topple it and continue the string. As you might have noticed, the seesaw uses two dominoes at each pivot point, (A, and B, and then D and E). This is to insure that the system remains intact after it has been set off. Figure 3-19 illustrates the movement of the dominoes to help you understand how this trick operates.

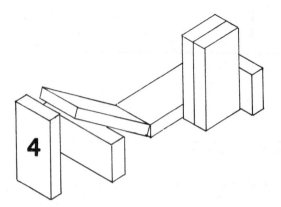

Corners

When you are setting up corner tricks, the distance between dominoes should increase as you approach and complete the corner. This will ensure that each domino hits the next one in line.

GRADUAL CORNER

Complexity: 1
POS: 5

The gradual corner is a domino trick that almost every one has done at one time or another. Figure 4-1 shows the proper setup.

SIDE STEP

Complexity: 1
POS: 5

The side step (Fig. 4-2) can be used in place of a gradual corner. When you are doing this trick, be careful not to side step more than three-fourths of a W or you might decrease the POS of the system.

ONE-DOMINO REVOLVING CORNER

Complexity: 2
POS: 5

With this trick (Fig. 4-3), a domino turns before it falls if the force on one side is not proportionally harder then the other side.

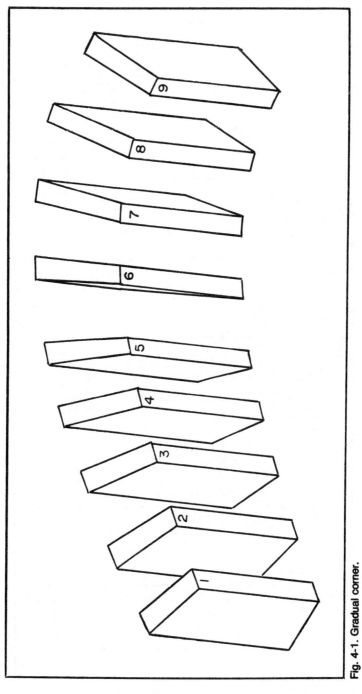

Fig. 4-1. Gradual corner.

63

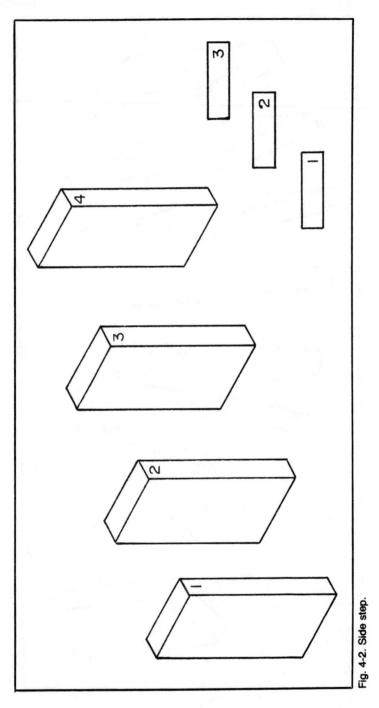

Fig. 4-2. Side step.

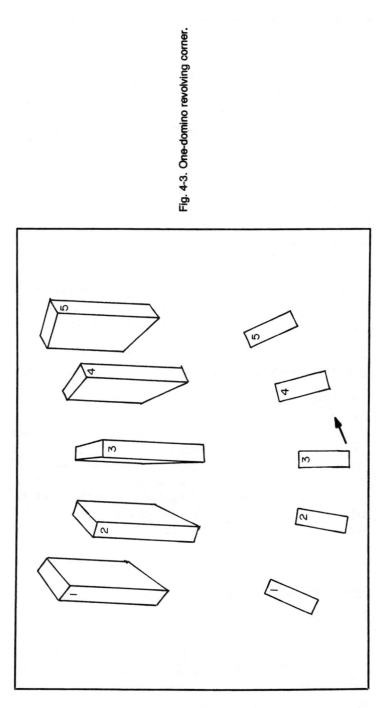

Fig. 4-3. One-domino revolving corner.

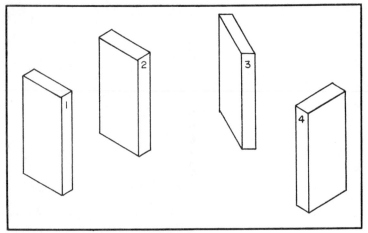

Fig. 4-4. Complex revolving corner.

Set domino 2 in such a relationship with domino 3 that, as it falls, it will hit only about one-third of domino 3's surface. In so doing, domino 3 will turn before it falls and continue the string almost every time.

COMPLEX REVOLVING CORNER

Complexity: 3
POS: 4

Refer to Figs. 4-4 and 4-5 to best understand how this corner trick works. It appears that as domino 2 is hit by domino 1, it would just fall over and not hit domino 3. But this does not happen! As in the previous trick, when domino 1 hits domino 2, it will rotate it as it falls over. The motion arrows show that, as domino 2 falls, it will hit domino 3 and set it rotating. This continues through the corner to complete the trick. This corner trick might be a little difficult to accomplish at first, but—with practice—it will be a dependable trick.

A 90-DEGREE SIDE WEDGE

Complexity: 2
POS: 4

A 90-degree corner trick (Fig. 4-6) is easily set up by placing domino 3 against dominoes 4 and 5 and then working both ways from there. Dominoes 4 and 5 are used to give enough support to domino

3 to hold it from falling. As domino 2 falls, it hits domino 3 on its leaning edge, and gives it enough power to push over dominoes 4 and 5 and to continue the string.

TURN AND FALL

Complexity: 2
POS: 4

As you can see in Fig. 4-7, this 90-degree corner trick is very simple to set up. What has basically been done is to take the one-domino revolving corner (Fig. 4-3) and reinforce it in such a way as to make it turn a complete 90 degrees.

Looking at the top view in Fig. 4-8, you can easily see that dominoes 1 and 2 are offset as if they were making a one-domino revolving corner. Also note that the domino marked A is against domino 2 in such a way as to hold the edge of domino 2 from moving. As domino 1 hits domino 2, domino A holds fast so as to make domino 2 swing around 90 degrees (as shown by the movement arrow in Fig. 4-8). When setting up this trick, note that domino A and domino 2 are against each other, and domino 1 hits only about one-third of domino 2.

A 90-DEGREE TOPPLE

Complexity: 2
POS: 3

Here is a 90-degree trick that does not look like a 90-degree trick. As you look at Figs. 4-9 and 4-10, you might not at first see how this trick could go around 90 degrees. Nevertheless, the

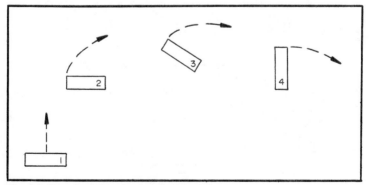

Fig. 4-5. Top view of a complex revolving corner.

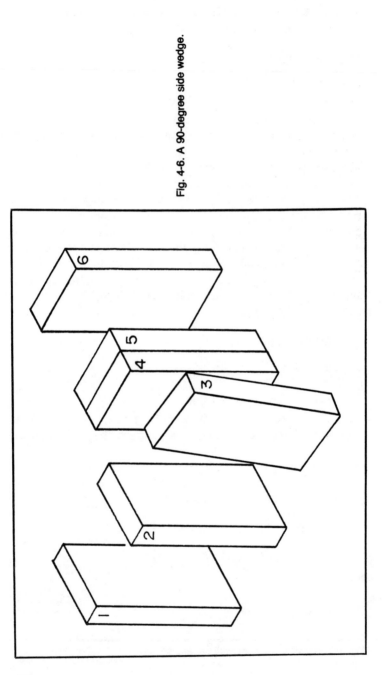

Fig. 4-6. A 90-degree side wedge.

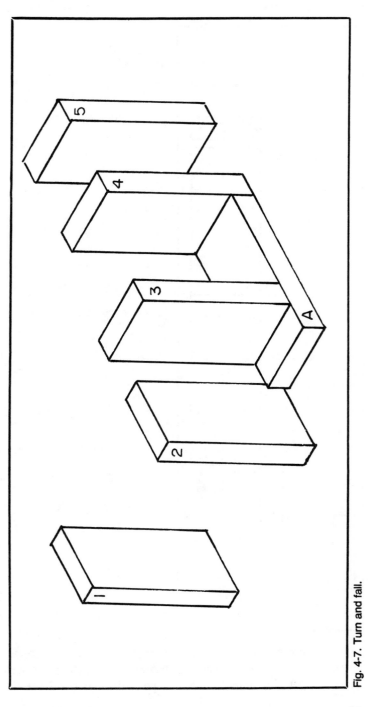

Fig. 4-7. Turn and fall.

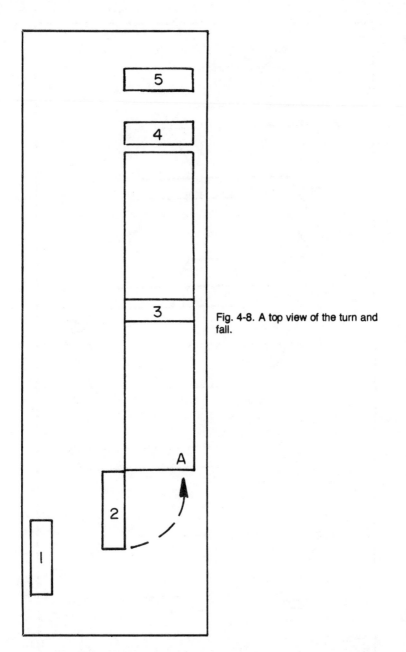

Fig. 4-8. A top view of the turn and fall.

operation of this system is really very simple. As power is applied to domino 1, it hits and knocks down domino 2, which then makes domino 3 fall as in a line. As this happens, domino 4 will lose its

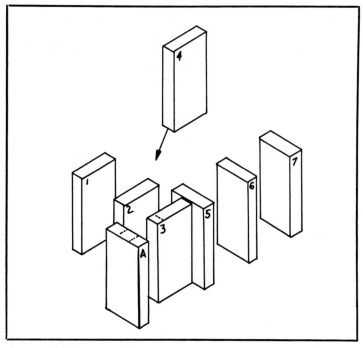

Fig. 4-9. A 90-topple.

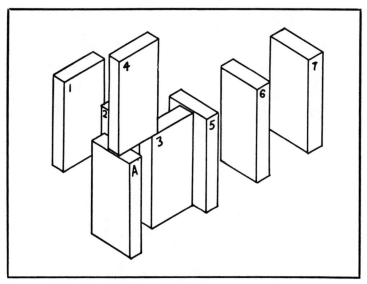

Fig. 4-10. A 90-topple completely assembled.

support from under one end and will fall to hit domino 5. Domino 5 will then continue the string to its completion.

As can be seen in Figs. 4-9 and 4-10, dominoes A and 3 are spaced apart by a distance of about one D. This will allow domino 4 to be set on top of dominoes A and 3.

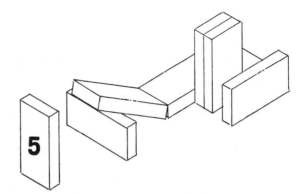

T's and 180-Degree Reversals

A *T*, as used in this book, is defined as a system in which there are two outputs that are each 90 degrees removed from the single input (as shown in Fig. 5-2). It is so named because, if you were to look straight down upon the system, it would look something like the letter T. This technique can be used anytime you want to branch off or expand a string.

A 180-degree reverser is a system in which its output is about in the opposite direction as its input. If you were to look down on a 180-degree reverser, it would appear that the string of dominoes came to a point before heading back in the same direction in which they came. This trick can be used in making pointed designs or if you want to use dominoes to write a word.

A DOUBLE WEDGE T

Complexity: 3
POS: 3

The dotted square and the arrow in Fig. 5-1 show that these parts are all moved up to the Y illustrated in Fig. 5-2. It can easily be seen that as the Y falls and starts to spread out, dominoes 3A and 3B will fall onto slanted dominoes. Domino 3A will hit domino A and domino 3B will hit domino C. As is shown by the movement arrows, these two dominoes will each fall down their slide unit. They each hit the domino at the bottom. Domino 3A will slide down domino A to hit 4A and domino 3B will slide down domino C to hit 4B.

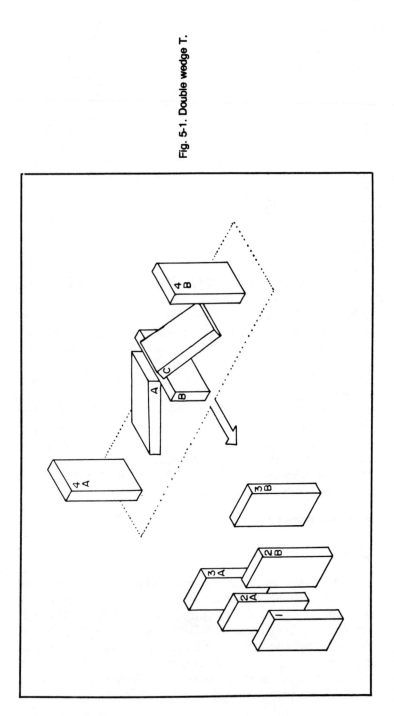

Fig. 5-1. Double wedge T.

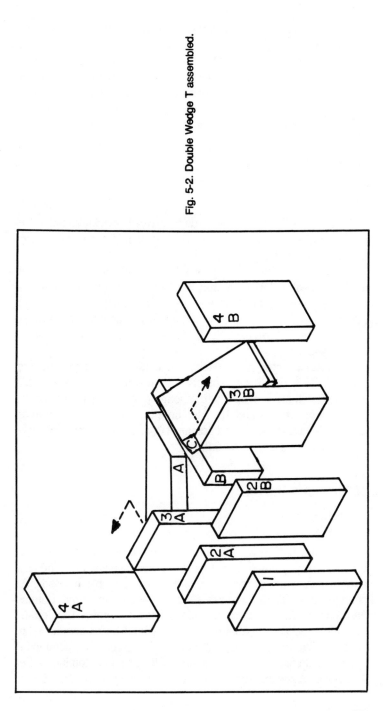

Fig. 5-2. Double Wedge T assembled.

As you are building this trick, you will have to space dominoes 3A and 3B about one H apart so that each will hit its slide domino at about its center. Also note that domino 4A is no more than one D away from domino A and that domino 4B is one D away from domino C. Domino 3A is set one W from domino A and domino 3B is one W from domino C with the trick set up as given. This trick will work 85 percent of the time.

DOUBLE TOPPLE T

Complexity: 3
POS: 3

Figure 5-3 shows two 90-degree topple tricks combined to give a double topple T. When domino 3 is hit and falls over, dominoes 4 and 4B will also fall.

Figure 5-4 shows that as 4A falls it will hit domino 5A and domino 4B will fall to hit domino 5B. Domino 4A's and domino 4B's movement arrows will help you understand how they cross each other as they fall. A front view of domino 4A and domino 4B would show that they cross each other much like the edges on a pair of cutting sheers.

A critical factor in this trick is the distance between dominoes 2 and 3. This should be about two D in order to guarantee that domino 2 will hit domino 3 with enough power to get it out of the way of dominoes 4A and 4B. Also note how domino 3 is set at an angle to hold domino 4A and domino 4B, and at the same time give each room to pass as they fall.

DOUBLE TURN AND FALL

Complexity: 3
POS: 4

For this trick (Fig. 5-5), simply take the turn and fall shown in Fig. 4-7 and expanded it by adding another turn and fall. The new trick will function in much the same way as its predecessor. As domino 2 falls, it hits dominoes 3A and 3B at the same time. Domino 3A then rotates, because of domino A, and hits domino 4A. Domino 3B rotates because of domino B and it will fall to hit domino 4B to continue that string. When you try this trick, make sure domino 3A is against domino A and that domino 3B is against domino B. Set dominoes 3A and 3B with a one-D space between them (Fig. 5-6).

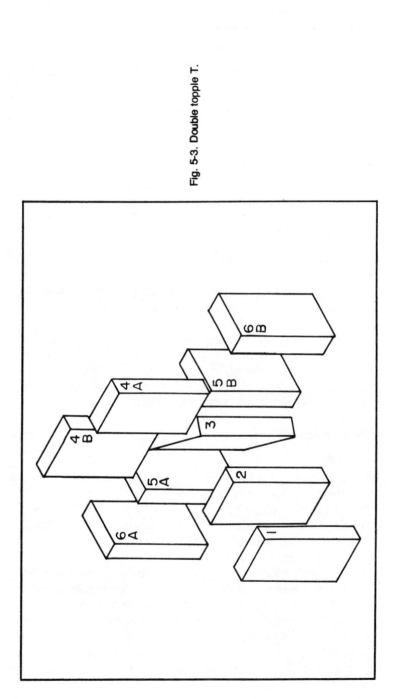

Fig. 5-3. Double topple T.

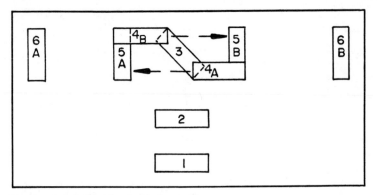

Fig. 5-4. A top view of a double topple T.

A COLLAPSING 180

Complexity: 1
POS: 4

Start on 180-degree reverses by taking on the simplest one that can be made. As a stand of two dominoes is hit by a single domino, the stand will fall on itself as is shown in Fig. 1-11. To take advantage of this, set the upper domino (4) on the lower one (3) in such a way that as domino 2 hits domino 3, domino 4 will fall a little to one side where you have strategically placed domino 5. This simple setup is shown in Fig. 5-7. Power will go in on domino 1 and with good fortune, it will come out on domino 6.

TABLE LEVER 180

Complexity: 2
POS: 2

Here is another way to complete a 180-degree reversal. As Figs. 5-8A and 5-8B show, domino 1 hits domino 2 as it falls over. Domino 2 will try to move backward, but it is held fast by domino A at its center. Therefore, domino 2 will start to rotate around domino A and act as a lever to push down domino 3 to continue the string.

The system shown in Fig. 5-8A and 5-8B works very well, but it does suffer from two small drawbacks. First, domino 2 sets on the table. Therefore, it "feels" the friction of the table as it is rotating. This makes the efficiency of the system very low and helps to lower its POS rating. Also, when domino 2 hits domino 3, it is pushing on its lower half. This too will lower the POS of this system. The next trick will solve both of these problems.

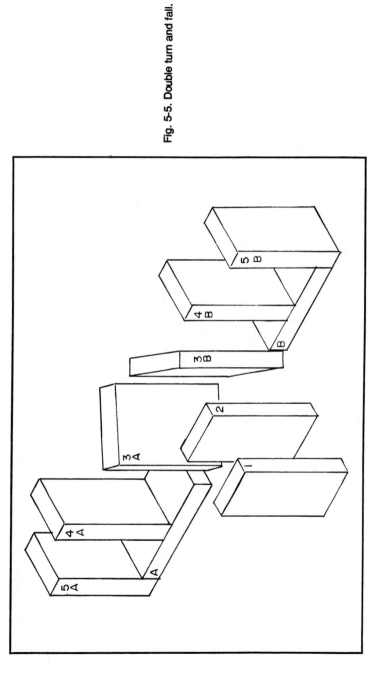

Fig. 5-5. Double turn and fall.

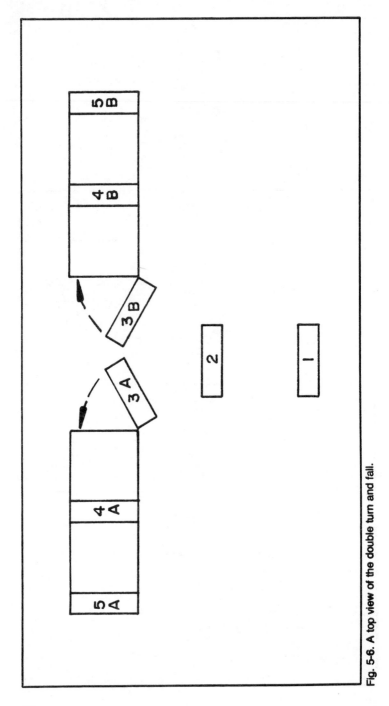

Fig. 5-6. A top view of the double turn and fall.

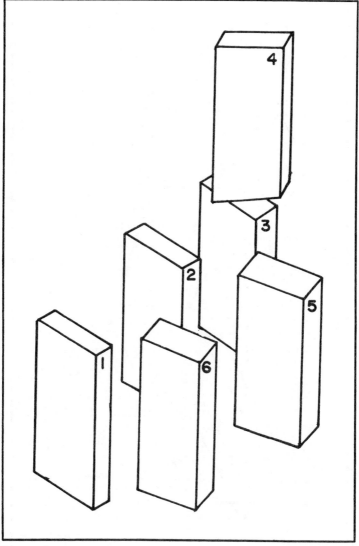

Fig. 5-7. Collapsing 180.

TOWER LEVER 180

Complexity: 2
POS: 5

This trick (Figs. 5-9A and 5-9B) takes the inefficient system of Figs. 5-8A and 5-8B and lifts it up to make it into a tower. The

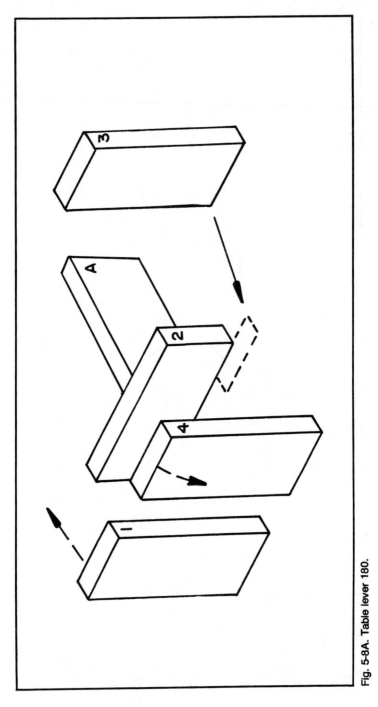

Fig. 5-8A. Table lever 180.

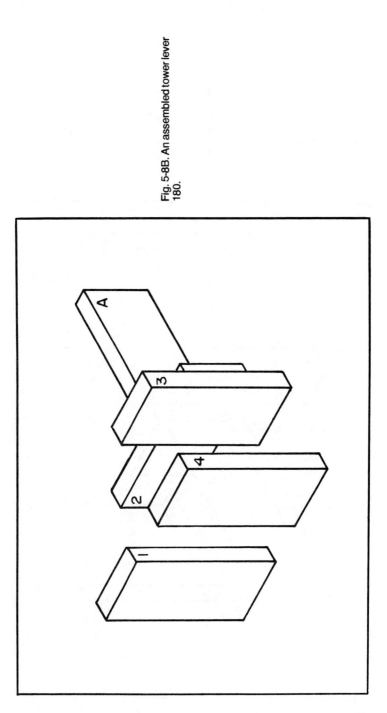

Fig. 5-8B. An assembled tower lever 180.

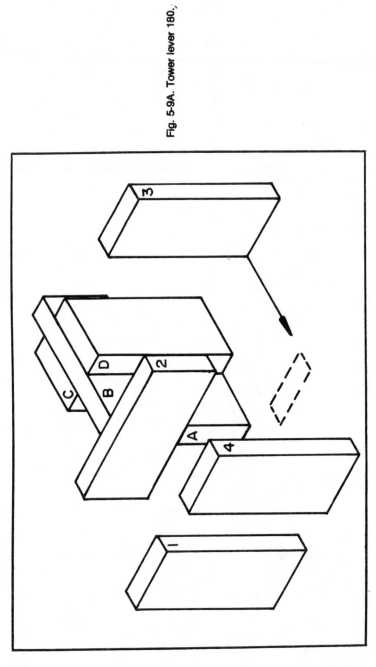

Fig. 5-9A. Tower lever 180.

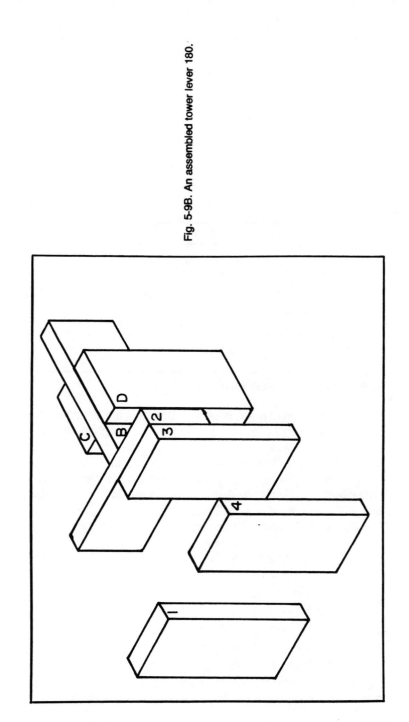

Fig. 5-9B. An assembled tower lever 180.

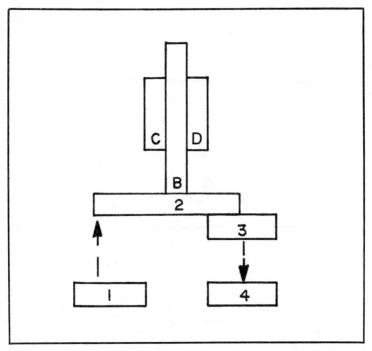

Fig. 5-10. A top view of a tower lever 180.

operation of the system is very simple. Domino 1 hits domino 2 and domino 2 rotates to hit domino 3. Domino 3 continues the string.

With this trick, all of the problems that plague the table lever 180 are eliminated. Domino 2 is no longer on the table. It is raised to set on domino A in such a way that it reduces friction to a minimum. Note that domino 2 now hits domino 3 on its top half; therefore, a lot less power is needed to tip it over.

Figure 5-10 shows the movement of the dominoes in this system. Also, note that dominoes C and D are used to help support domino B on top of domino A. You now have a very versatile tower 180 that can be used for many different tricks.

COMPLEX ZIGZAG

Complexity: 2
POS: 5

Use the tower lever 180 (Fig. 5-9) to make a complex zigzag. Figure 5-11 shows a top view of the complete system. Note that there are three tower lever 180's to reverse the direction of the

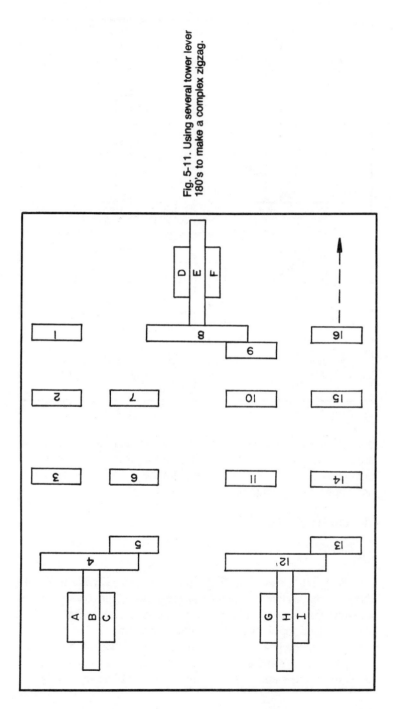

Fig. 5-11. Using several tower lever 180's to make a complex zigzag.

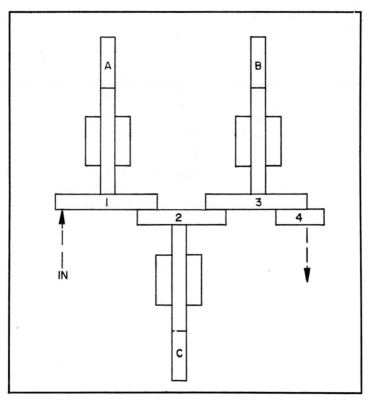

Fig. 5-12. The simple zigzag.

dominoes as they go back and forth in the system. The tower 180's are made up of dominoes A through I, with the lever dominoes being dominoes 4, 8, and 12. Power goes into the system with domino 1 and comes out through domino 16.

THE SIMPLE ZIGZAG

Complexity: 2
POS: 4

With this system (Fig. 5-12), the complex zigzag is simplified. Simply remove all of the dominoes from between the towers to give a faster operating system with a whole new effect. Figure 5-12 shows a good top view of the complete system.

The power goes in by a domino falling against domino 1. Domino 1 rotates and pushes against domino 2—and so on—until domino 3 rotates and topples domino 4 to continue the string.

Note that the dominoes A, B, and C are not used in previous towers. These dominoes stand on end behind the tower to reinforce it so that it will not move backward. This system is so efficient that the process of adding towers could go on to approximately eight towers in a row. This can be a very impressive trick.

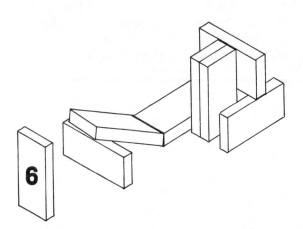

Special Effects and Safety Valves

This chapter is a catch-all for tricks that do not fit in other chapters. The majority of these tricks are not very spectacular by themselves, but they can be impressive when used in conjunction with other tricks.

SIDE-FALL CONTINUATION

Complexity: 2
POS: 5

This simple trick ends with dominoes A and B left standing. As you can see in Fig. 6-1, domino 1 hits domino 2 which then falls between dominoes A and B to continue the string by hitting domino 3. This trick is not much by itself, but you will be able to use dominoes A and B at a later time.

SIDE-SLIDE CONTINUATION

Complexity: 1
POS: 5

This trick is basically the same as that shown in Fig. 6-1. Here domino 1 falls to hit, and then slide, dominoes 2 and 3. Domino 3 then passes over domino 4 to continue the string by hitting domino 5. As you can see in Fig. 6-2, dominoes 2 and 3 will remain standing after the trick is over. This is a very good trick for making figure 8's (shown in Fig. 6-3).

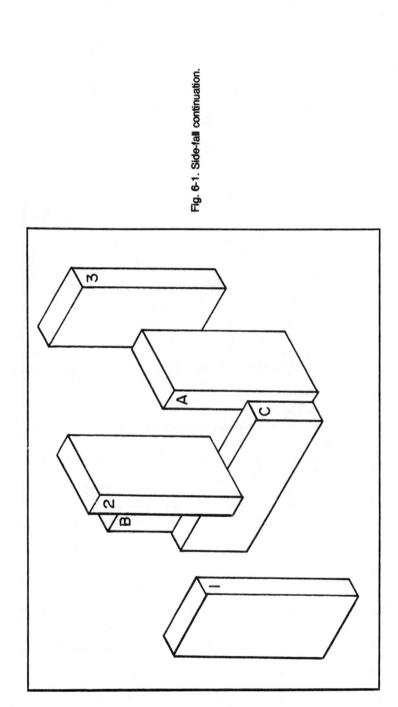

Fig. 6-1. Side-fall continuation.

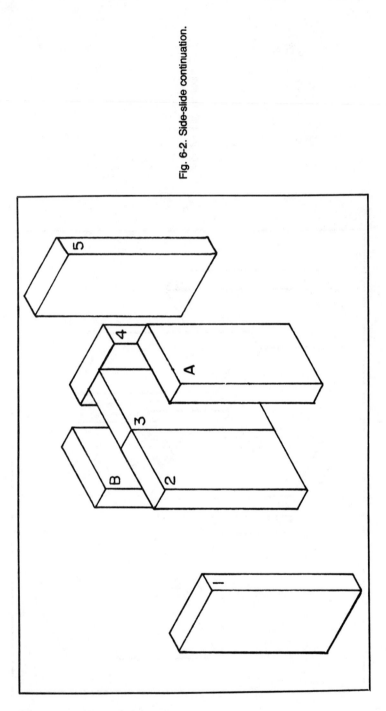

Fig. 6-2. Side-slide continuation.

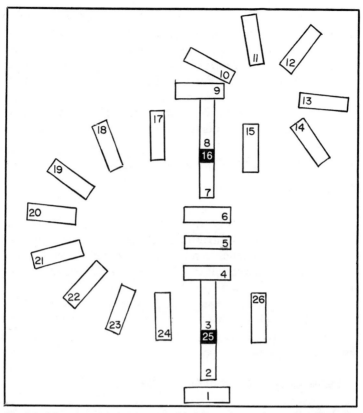

Fig. 6-3. A top view showing how the side fall can be used to make a figure 8.

FIGURE 8'S

Complexity: 2
POS: 4

Figure 6-3 shows how the side-slide continuation can be used to make a figure 8. Power goes to domino 1 and continues through the string to come out at domino 26. Note that domino 7 is also numbered 16 because it is used twice as part of the side-slide continuation. Domino 2 is also numbered 25.

SIMPLE FALLING FORWARD CONVERTER
Complexity: 3
POS: 4

As the name implies, this system will convert the downward power of a falling domino into the forward motion of a string of falling dominoes. This system could be used to continue the string from a table (or high surface) to a floor or a low surface.

When going from table to floor, the last domino on the table should be set at the edge so as to fall off and to hit any one of the four dominoes numbered 1 in Fig. 6-4. This domino will transmit its power to either of the dominoes numbered 2 and will thus continue the string. The biggest drawback for this converter is that the target area can be missed if you drop the domino any great distance.

DEPENDABLE FALLING FORWARD CONVERTER

Complexity: 3
POS: 4

With this trick (Fig. 6-5), the target area of the simple converter (Fig. 6-4) is expanded to make the converter more dependable. If the falling domino hits only one of the dominoes numbered 1, its power will be converted to a forward movement. Dominoes 2 and 3 will fall and continue the string. Note that this trick can be expanded even further by adding more strings of number 1 dominoes. If this is done, you will have to add an equal number of number 2 and 3 to reduce the target to a single forward string of dominoes.

SEESAW FALLING FORWARD CONVERTER

Complexity: 3
POS: 4

With this converter (Fig. 6-6), notice that the target—consisting of number 1 dominoes—has been raised and put on supports. This system is about as efficient as the last converter. It is included to show that there is always more than one way to achieve a desired result.

SIMPLE ONE-WAY VALVE

Complexity: 3
POS: 4

Here is an idea that can come in very handy when you begin to set up a string of tricks. The one-way valve (Fig. 6-7) is so-named because it will allow the string of dominoes to fall in one direction, but not in the reverse direction. This is handy in preventing an accidental "tripping" of the preceding trick and destroying a lot of

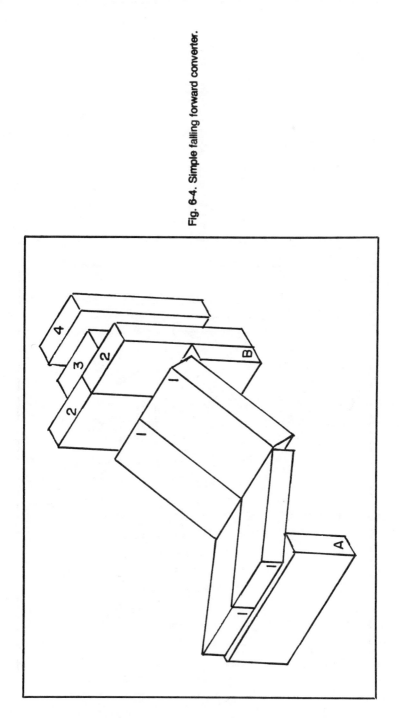

Fig. 6-4. Simple falling forward converter.

95

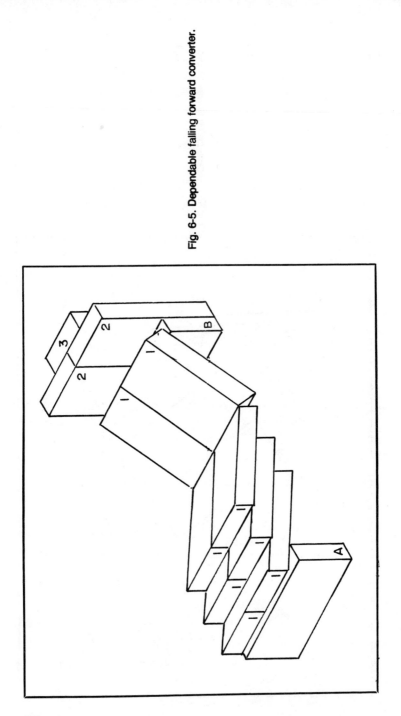

Fig. 6-5. Dependable falling forward converter.

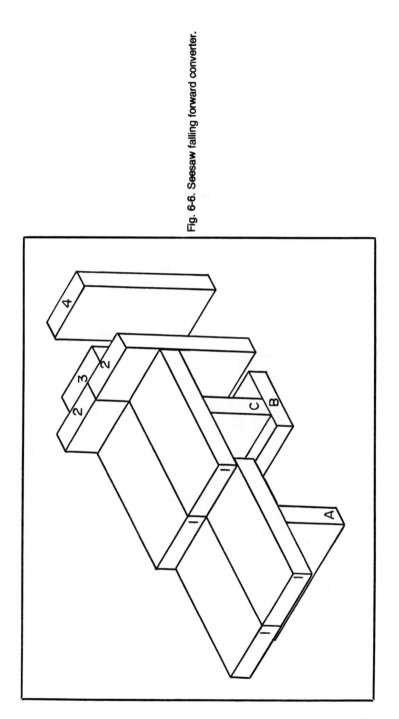

Fig. 6-6. Seesaw falling forward converter.

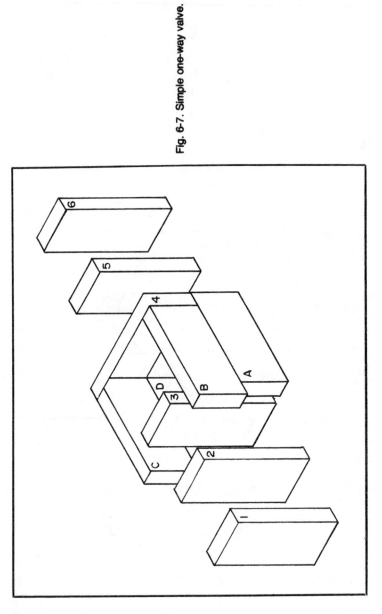

Fig. 6-7. Simple one-way valve.

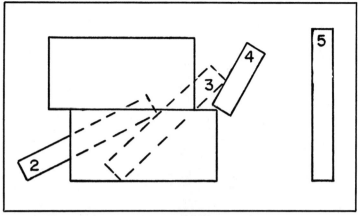

Fig. 6-8. The forward forces in the simple one-way valve.

hard work. The valve can be left right in the string as the string is set off. This eliminates the need for going back and adding dominoes to a blank space. Figure 6-8 shows the valve in its forward movement. As you can see, domino 2 will hit domino 3 which, in turn, will hit domino 4 off its supports to hit domino 5 to continue the string.

Figure 6-9 shows what will happen if by chance the string is set off falling backward. The falling dominoes would come in from the right to hit and knock down domino 5. Domino 5 would hit domino 4 and go no further. Domino 4 will be held fast in place by supporting dominoes.

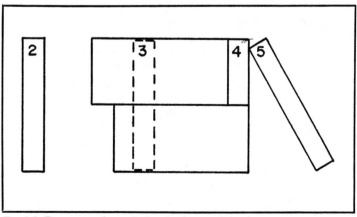

Fig. 6-9. The reverse forces in the simple one-way valve.

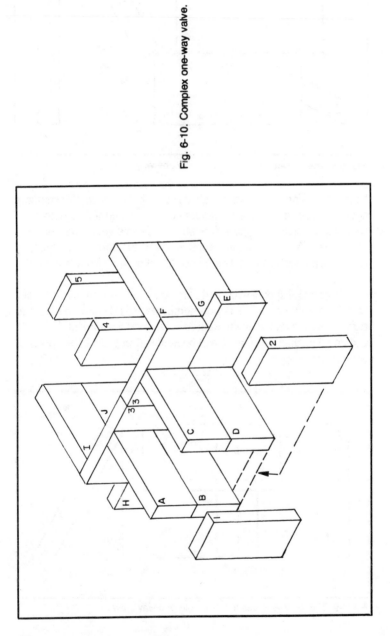

Fig. 6-10. Complex one-way valve.

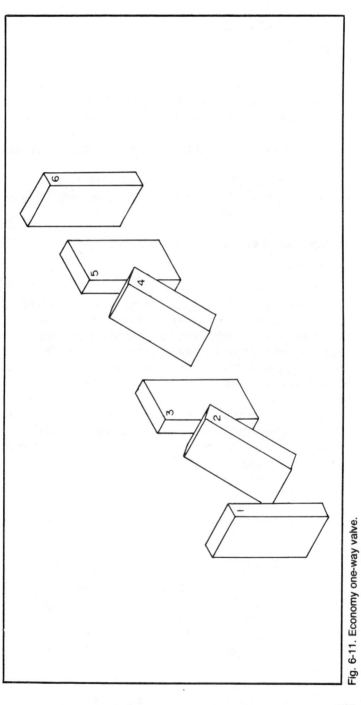

Fig. 6-11. Economy one-way valve.

COMPLEX ONE-WAY VALVE

Complexity: 4
POS: 4

This trick (Fig. 6-10) is also a one-way valve and it serves the same function as the valve shown in Fig. 6-7. For this valve, power is applied to domino 1. It hits and knocks down domino 2 which, in turn, falls through the number 3 dominoes like going through a swinging-bar door. Dominoes 2 and 3 then hit domino 4 to continue the string.

If there is an accident and dominoes 4 and 5 fall backward, they will be held fast by the number 3 dominoes. The remainder of the setup will be saved from distruction.

ECONOMY ONE-WAY VALVE

Complexity: 3
POS: 4

Believe it or not, the system shown in Fig. 6-11 is the simplest one-way valve. In the forward direction, domino 1 hits domino 2, which then pushes domino 3 over. Domino 3 falls to hit 4, which then pushes domino 5 over to continue the forward string. In the reverse direction, domino 6 falls backward to hit domino 5. In most cases, domino 5 will try to push domino 4 over its center of gravity—but it will not succeed.

If by chance, domino 4 does go over to hit domino 3, it will have lost so much power that it will not hit domino 3 hard enough to move domino 2 any great distance. This way the trick is saved from distruction by the valve.

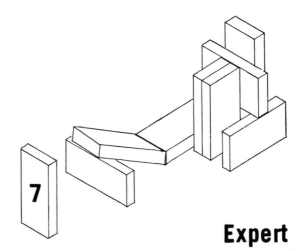

Expert

Some of the tricks described in this chapter have a low POS. Don't get discouraged if you can't get them to work without a "few" trial runs.Understanding how the tricks should work is the only way you will get these tricks to function. Read the instructions carefully and make any minor adjustment as needed to make the trick work. Use your common sense to help get any kinks out of your tricks. Variables that you will have to deal with include the size and weight of the dominoes, the friction of the playing surface, and the relationship of the width to the height and depth of the domino.

COMPLEX SIDE FLIP

Complexity: 3
POS: 3

This trick (Fig. 7-1) starts by leading the input power through dominoes 2 and 3. As domino 3 falls forward, it hits domino 4 on its forward flat surface. Domino 4 then acts as a lever to flip domino 5 through the air to hit domino 6 and continue the string. Make sure domino 1 is spaced about one W from dominoes 2 and A (as shown). Also make certain that dominoes A and B are against each other to give proper spacing to the rest of the trick.

FORWARD TUMBLE

Complexity: 3
POS: 3

With this trick, there are a number of supporting dominoes used to lift dominoes 2 and 3 in a step-like structure (Fig. 7-2). In

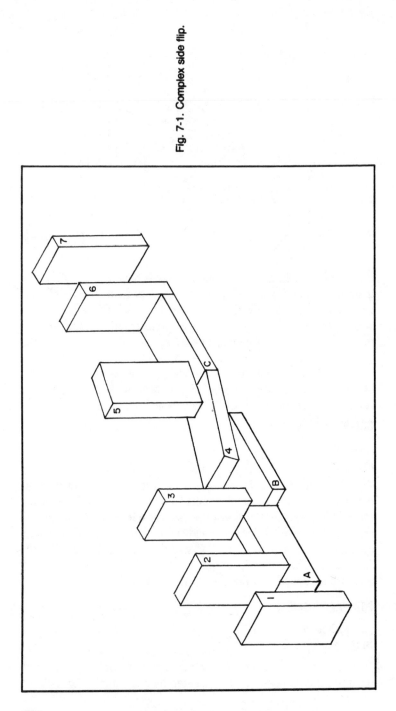

Fig. 7-1. Complex side flip.

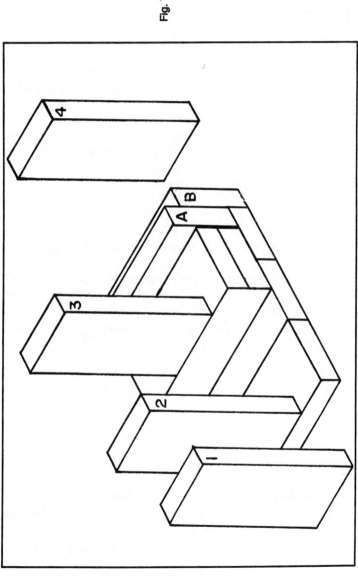

Fig. 7-2. Forward tumble.

Fig. 7-3, domino 1 is knocked over to hit domino 2 which, in turn, knocks over domino 3. Domino 3 then tumbles over the short wall of domino A (as shown by the movement arrow).

It is important to keep domino 1 at about one W from domino 2. Also, note that domino 4 is spaced about one H from domino B and that it is in a straight line with dominoes 1, 2, and 3.

DROP AND DOUBLE FLIP

Complexity: 3
POS: 3

As shown in Fig. 7-4, the input at domino 1 branches out to give a *domino dropper*. As domino 4 falls, it hits domino 5 and sets it rotating like a lever to throw domino 6 over its center of gravity. Domino 6 then hits domino 7 and it, in turn, throws domino 8 over its center of gravity. Domino 8 then hits domino 9 to provide an output to continue other tricks. Figure 7-6 shows the movement arrows for this system. Note that input dominoes 1, 2A, 2B, 3A, 3B, and 4 are left out to help simplify this view.

The best way to set up this trick is to balance domino 7 on domino C and then place domino 8 and domino 7 and domino D. Note that only a small part of domino 8 is sitting on domino 7. This will make balancing domino 7 and domino 8 a whole lot easier.

Domino B is set on it's side at a distance of one H from domino C. Domino A is spaced at W and D from domino B. Dominoes 5 and 6 can then be balanced on dominoes A and B. Now add dominoes 3A, 3B, and 4. Make sure that domino 3A and domino 3B are turned outward so as not to hit domino A. Also make sure you do not drop domino 4; this will trigger the system and you will be back to step one.

With the system complete, the input of dominoes 1, 2A, and 2B can be added. The output of domino 9 will continue the series of tricks. Figure 7-5 shows the system completely set up.

THE FORWARD BASE FLICK

Complexity: 4
POS: 4

The name for this trick (Fig. 7-7) is derived from the action of domino 3 as it is flicked forward in a fast motion. Domino 1 hits the end of domino 2 in such a way that it pushes the base of domino 3 in a forward direction. The top of domino 3 is held in place by being against domino D.

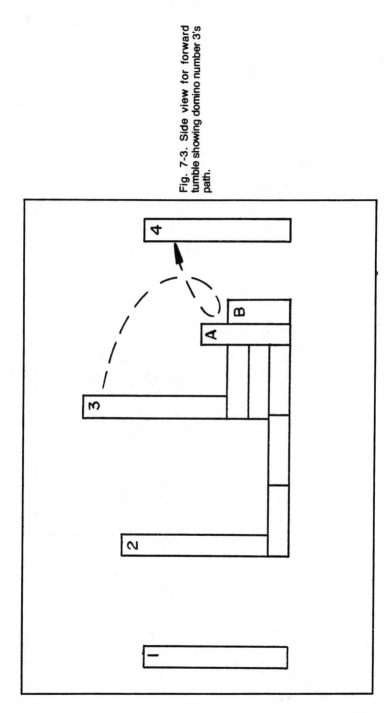

Fig. 7-3. Side view for forward tumble showing domino number 3's path.

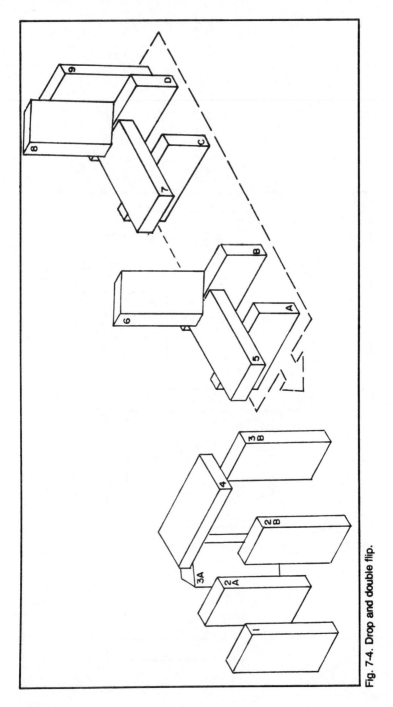

Fig. 7-4. Drop and double flip.

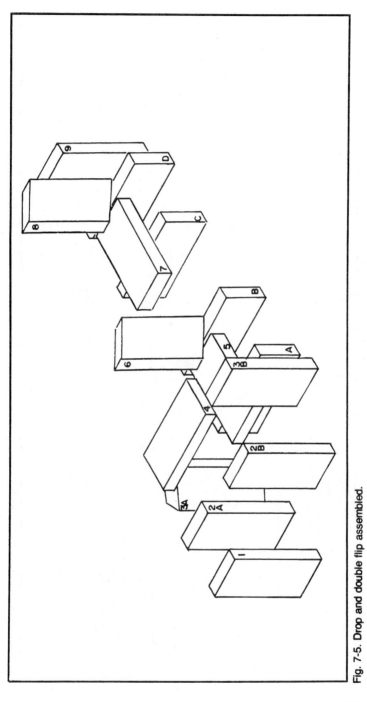

Fig. 7-5. Drop and double flip assembled.

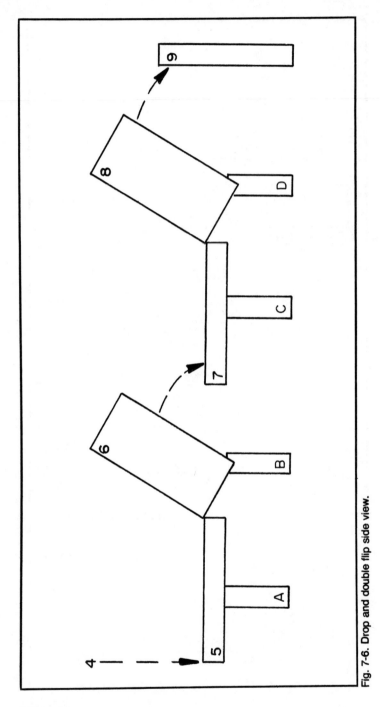

Fig. 7-6. Drop and double flip side view.

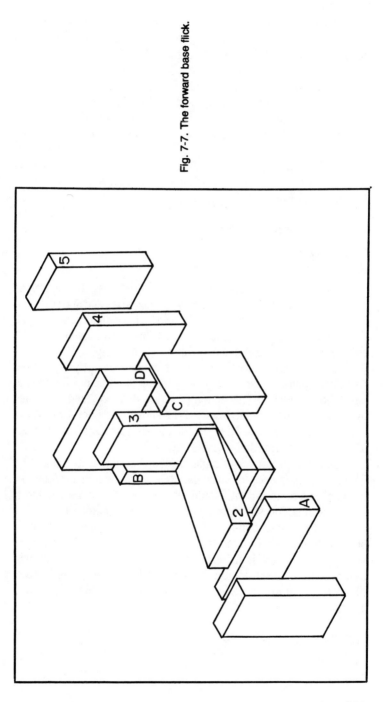

Fig. 7-7. The forward base flick.

Because of this, domino 3 rotates (see the movement arrow in Fig. 7-8). The base of domino 3 then hits the upper half of domino 4 to tip it over and continue the string.

This trick is set up as follows. The two supporting dominoes are laid face down. Dominoes B and C are stood along side in such a way that their edges line up with the ends of the supporting dominoes. Domino D is then set on dominoes B and C close to the rear edges of these dominoes. Domino 3 is then set up between dominoes B and C, and dominoes 2, A, and 1 are set up so that domino 2 is up against domino 3 and domino 1 will hit the end of domino 2. Domino 4 is set at less than one D from dominoes B and C (as shown in Figure 7-8).

COMPLEX ROUNDABOUT 90

Complexity: 5
POS: 3

This trick is made up of many of the operations previously used only once per trick. Domino 1 hits domino 2 on its end and transfers its power to domino 3 (Fig. 7-9). Domino 3 is against domino 4 and, as it slides, it pushes domino 4 out from under domino 5. The relationship of these dominoes can be seen in Fig. 7-10.

As domino 5 loses its support, it rotates to an upright position. As this happens, domino 6, which is on top of dominoes 5 and 7, is pushed by domino 5. This action tips over domino 7 and continues the string to the output. Figure 7-11 shows the operation of the second half of this trick. Note that dominoes 1 through 3 are left out of this illustration to help simplify it.

This trick is not very simple to set up because of its instability. The easiest sequence for setting it up is as follows. Place domino 5 on domino 4 so that it will stand by itself. Add dominoes A and B behind domino 5 as shown in Fig. 7-11. These dominoes are used as supports to prevent domino 5 from staying on top of domino 4 as it slides by domino 3. Dominoes 7 and 6 can now be added. Figure 7-9 shows how domino 7 is set up against domino 4 so that domino 6 will reach the tops of both dominoes 5 and 7. Add the rest of the system. Make sure that domino 8 is against domino 3 and that domino 3 is against domino 4.

THE PUSH, FALL, SLIDE 90

Complexity: 4
POS: 3

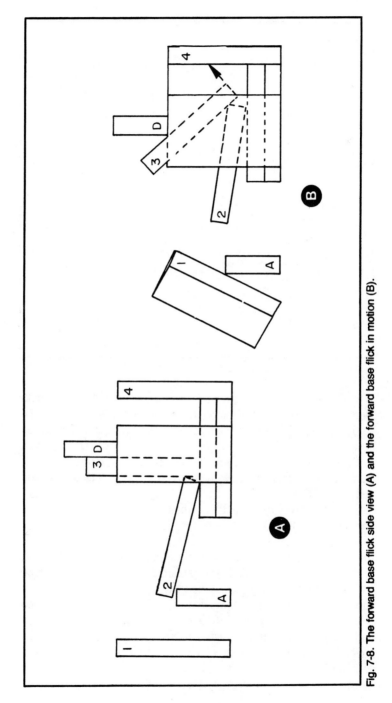

Fig. 7-8. The forward base flick side view (A) and the forward base flick in motion (B).

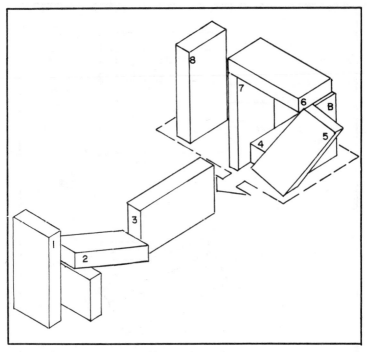

Fig. 7-9. Complex roundabout 90.

This is the most complex 90-degree corner trick in this book. Domino 1 hits domino 2; domino 2, in turn, slides dominoes 3 and 4 so that domino 5 looses its support and falls. Domino 6 then slides down domino 5 to hit domino 7 to continue the string. Dominoes A, B, C, and D are used as stops to hold domino 5 as domino 4 slides out from under it. Note the movement arrows in Fig. 7-12 to help you understand this operation.

The best way to set up this complex trick is to start by placing dominoes 3, 4, E, and 5 as shown in Fig. 7-12. Dominoes A, B, C, and D are added to the system to give support to domino 5. Note that these four dominoes are set very close to dominoes 3 and 4. Next, dominoes 6 and 7 are added. The remainder of the dominoes can be added without any problem. When the system is set up, double check to see if everything is ready to go. Make sure that there is no space between dominoes 2, 3, and 4. If too much of domino 4 is under domino 5, domino 4 will not receive enough power to be pushed clear. For this reason, hold dominoes C and D with one hand as you slide dominoes 2, 3, and 4 forward until domino 5 is only setting on about one-fourth D of domino 4.

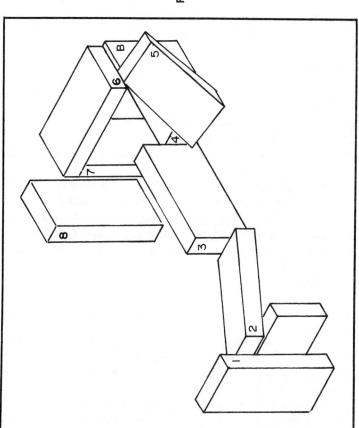

Fig. 7-10. Complex roundabout 90 assembled.

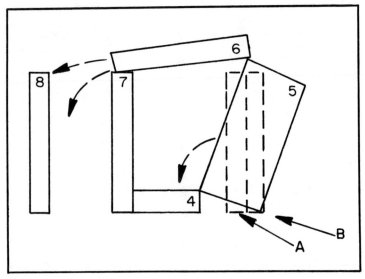

Fig. 7-11. Side view of roundabout 90.

THE PUSH, FALL, SLIDE T

Complexity: 4
POS: 3

This trick is an expansion of the basic push, fall, and slide into a complex T (Fig. 7-15). Note that Fig. 7-16 has just three more dominoes than Fig. 7-13. The three new dominoes are shown in Fig. 7-17; they are dominoes 6B, 7B, and 8B.

The operation of this system is almost the same as the push, fall, and slide 90. The exception is that as domino 5 falls it also drops domino 6B. Figure 7-17 shows that as 6B drops it pushes domino 7B over to continue the string. In setting up this trick, it is best to set up the push, fall, and slide 90, and then add dominoes 7B, 8B, and 6B.

DOWN THE CHUTE

Complexity: 3
POS: 3

This is a very interesting trick; don't pass it up. Note that Fig. 7-18 shows the down the chute system from a rear view. This view best shows the operation of the system. Domino B forms a chute down which domino 6 can fall.

The system works as follows. Dominoes 1, 2, 3, and 4 raise the power of the input to the top of the tower to where domino 4 hits

116

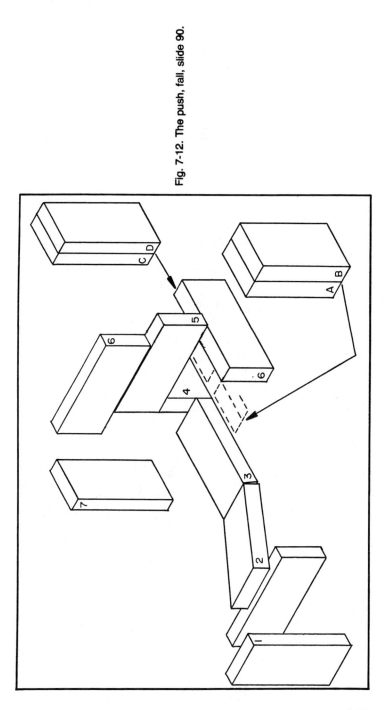

Fig. 7-12. The push, fall, slide 90.

117

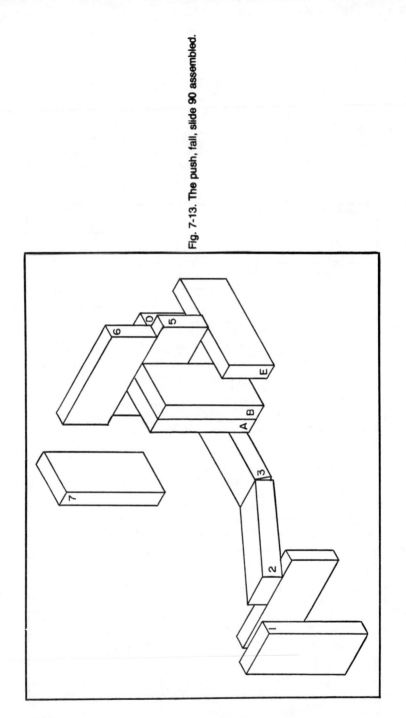

Fig. 7-13. The push, fall, slide 90 assembled.

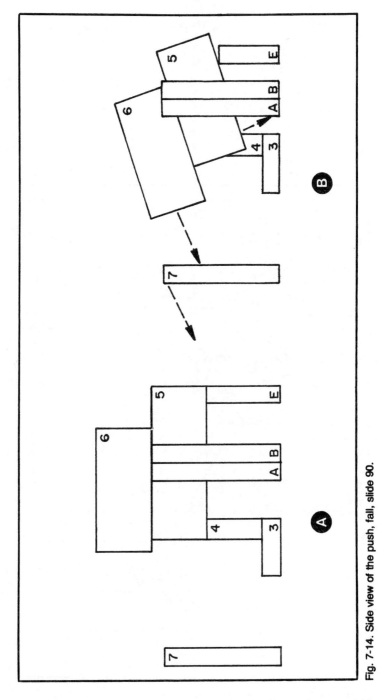

Fig. 7-14. Side view of the push, fall, slide 90.

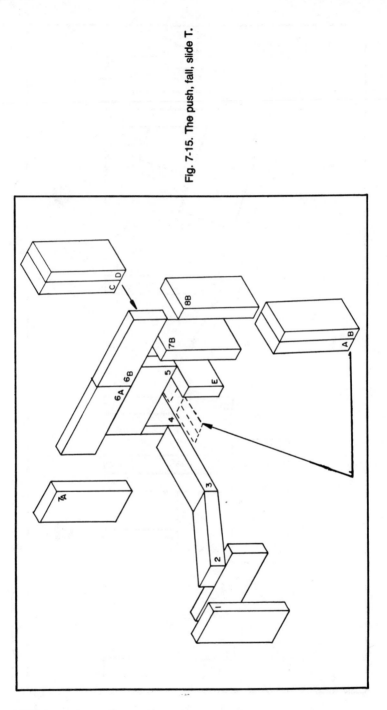

Fig. 7-15. The push, fall, slide T.

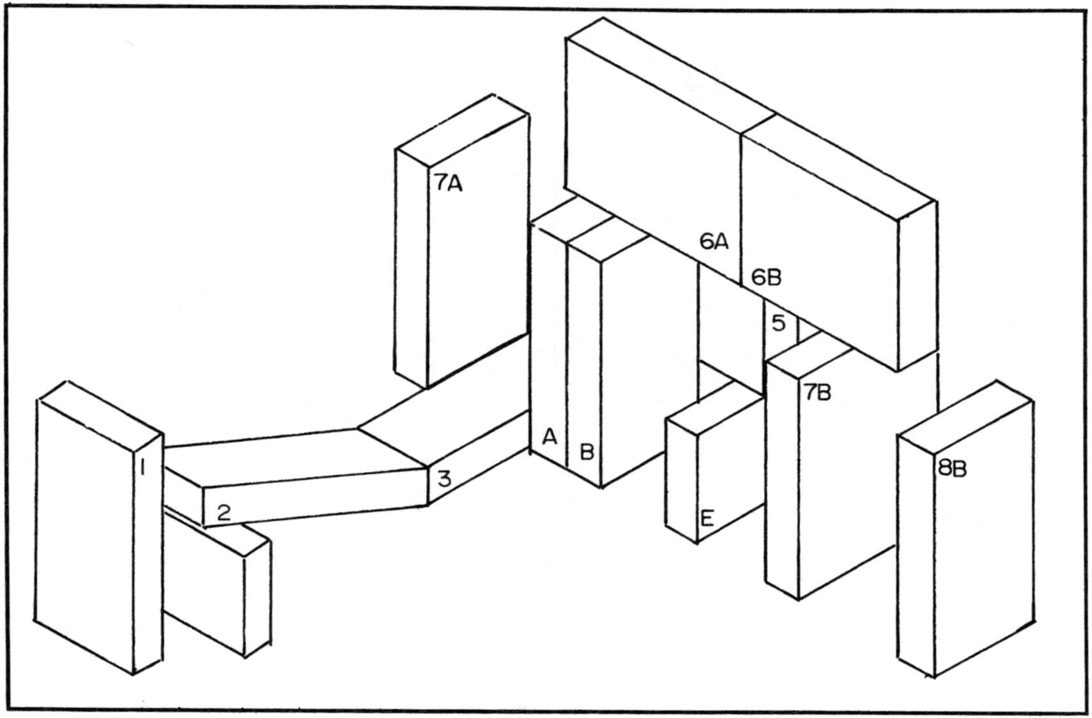

Fig. 7-16. The push, fall, slide T assembled.

121

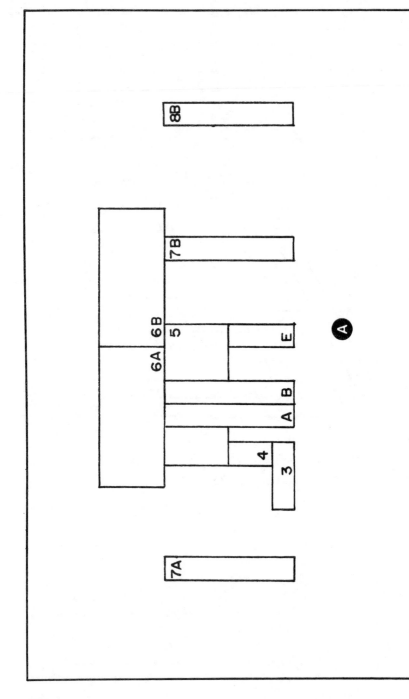

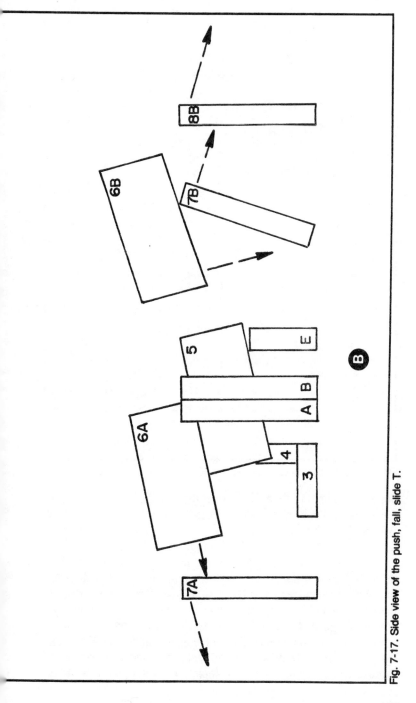

Fig. 7-17. Side view of the push, fall, slide T.

123

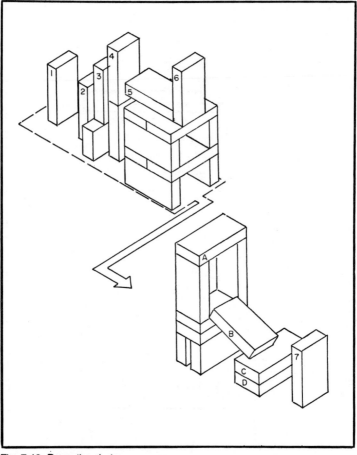

Fig. 7-18. Down the chute.

domino 5. Domino 5 then slides to hit the base of domino 6. Domino 6's top is held in place by domino A (see Fig. 6-20). The bottom of domino 6 is then pushed off the platform. It falls and slides down domino B, and hits domino 7 to complete the string.

The best way to set up this system is to compare Figs. 7-18 through 7-20 in order to set up all the unmarked dominoes. After this is done, dominoes C and D are placed one W from the foot of the tower. Domino B is set at an angle to make the chute. Note that domino B is placed so that its lower end is setting only on domino C at a distance of about one D. This will ensure that domino B is set at the proper angle. Dominoes A and 7 are then added. Dominoes 1 through 6 can now be added to complete the setup of this system.

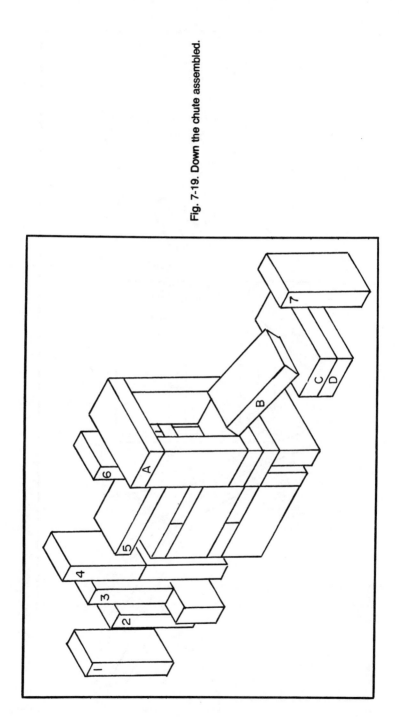

Fig. 7-19. Down the chute assembled.

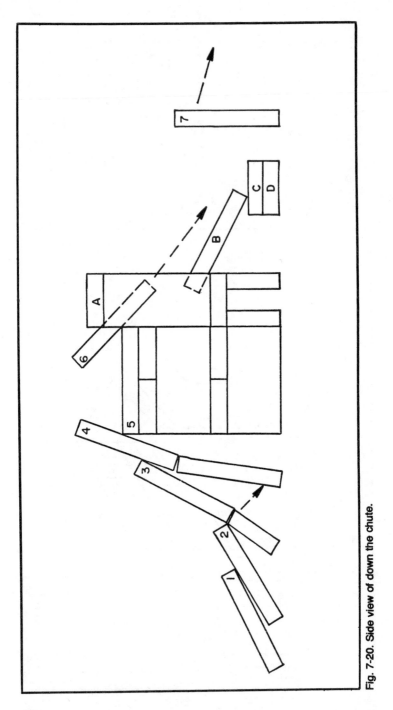

Fig. 7-20. Side view of down the chute.

Before you try to start this system, first make sure that everything is set to go. With one hand, slide domino 5 forward and the base of domino 6 forward until domino 6 is on the platform by only one-half a D. The other hand can be used to hold domino A in place. This is done to insure that domino 6 will fall when it is pushed by domino 5.

Now the system is all ready to go. Note that the tower structure will remain in one piece after the trick has been completed.

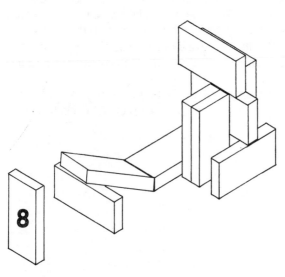

Big Endings

The systems described in this chapter can be used to end a string of tricks. All of these tricks have one input and no output. The idea is to make as big a bang as possible.

THE DISTANCE FALL

Complexity: 1
POS: 5

The idea behind this ending is to make domino 7 (Fig. 8-1) fall through the air as far as possible. With this system, domino 7 can fall up to about 2½ feet. As shown in Fig. 8-1, there is a one D space between each stand of dominoes. This is done to make the system very unstable. It will easily fall over when it is hit by domino 3.

THE TOWER FALL

Complexity: 2
POS: 4

Here is a tower that will fall over as it is hit by the incoming domino 1. Figures 8-2 and 8-3 show how to set up this trick. Note that the center line of domino A is lined up with one edge of domino B. This will make domino B hold most of the weight of the tower.

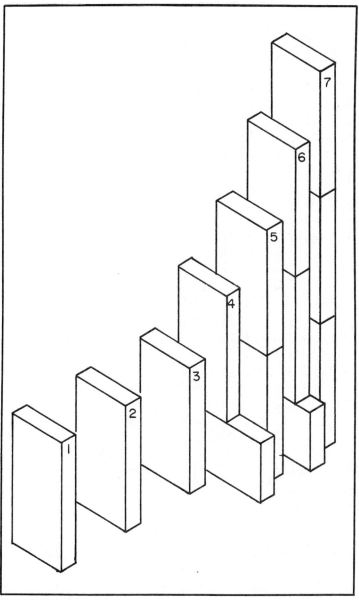

Fig. 8-1. The distance fall.

Domino 3 is under domino A in such a way as to steady the tower. Domino 3 does not hold much of the tower's weight. As domino 2 hits domino 3, domino 3 will fall out from under domino A and the

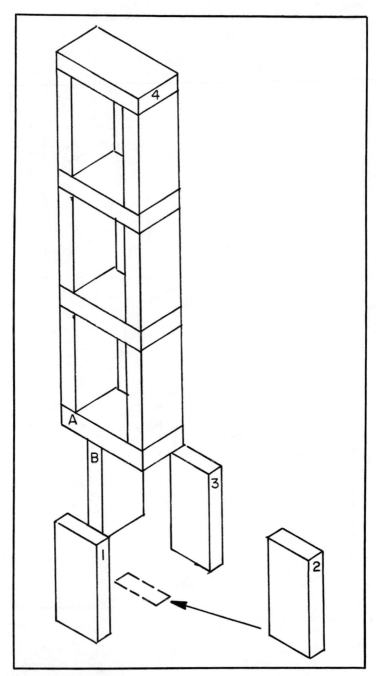

Fig. 8-2. The tower fall.

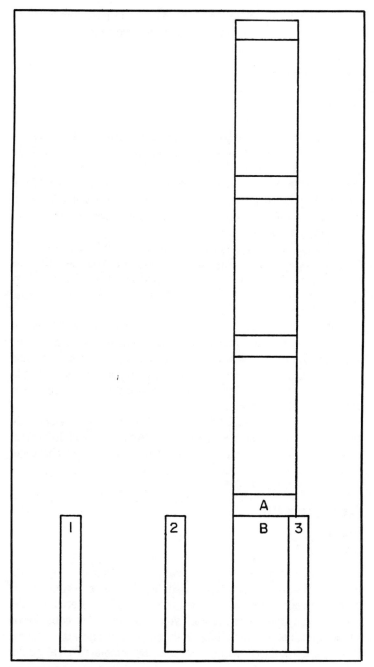

Fig. 8-3. The tower fall side view.

tower will fall over. Note that domino 2 is not under domino A and that domino 3 is under domino A by only two-thirds of a D.

THE TOWER DIVER

Complexity: 4
POS: 3

This trick is called the tower diver (Fig. 8-4) because it includes one domino on top of a tower that will dive off and provide a big finish. As shown in Fig. 8-5, the complete tower is set at an angle. This is done to make domino 5 become very unstable, it should be at the verge of falling. As dominoes 1 through 4 fall over, they will pick up enough power to hit the tower and cause domino 5 to become unbalanced and fall.

The system can easily be set up as shown in Figs. 8-4 and 8-5. At first, do not set up dominoes 1 through 4. You must find the critical angle of the tower before the trick will work. The best way to do this is to pick one domino—such as domino 5—and use it with the same end up every time.

Start with the tower at a more or less level state and set domino 5 on top right on the edge. With your left hand, place one finger on domino A and your thumb on domino B. Your right hand can be used to slowly push the tower by dominoes D and E up on to dominoes A and B. This will slowly increase the angle of tilt of the tower until domino 5 falls.

At this point, reverse the movement and reduce the angle until the domino will just balance on the tower. Add the rest of the system as shown. The trick can then be set off with a good chance of working.

THE ZIGZAG WALL

Complexity: 2
POS: 4

Here is a wall of dominoes that can be set up as a big ending. Figure 8-6 shows a fairly small wall, but this same system can be expanded upon to provide as big a wall as you like. Because of the relative high stability of the wall, you must use a Y to come in and set both ends of the wall falling. Figure 8-7 shows how this is done. If you were to knock down only one end, the complete wall might not fall.

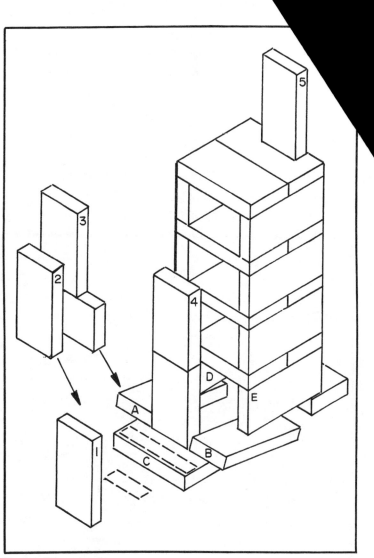

Fig. 8-4. The tower diver.

THE COLLAPSIBLE WALL

Complexity: 2
POS: 4

The wall for this trick (Fig. 8-9) is a variation of the wall shown in Fig. 8-6. Everything about Fig. 8-6 holds true for the wall shown in Fig. 8-8. The only difference is that the wall shown in Fig. 8-6 is

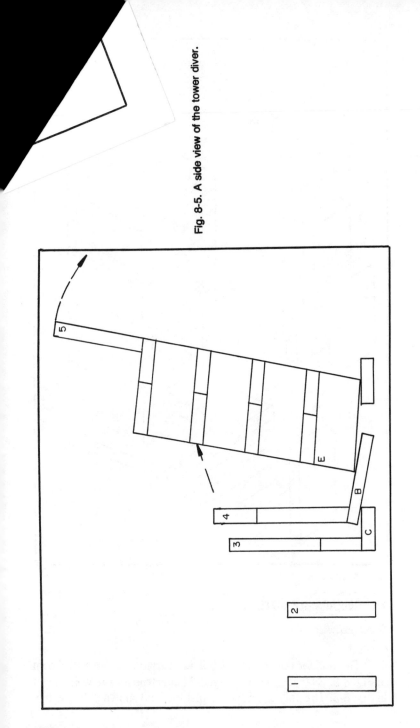

Fig. 8-5. A side view of the tower diver.

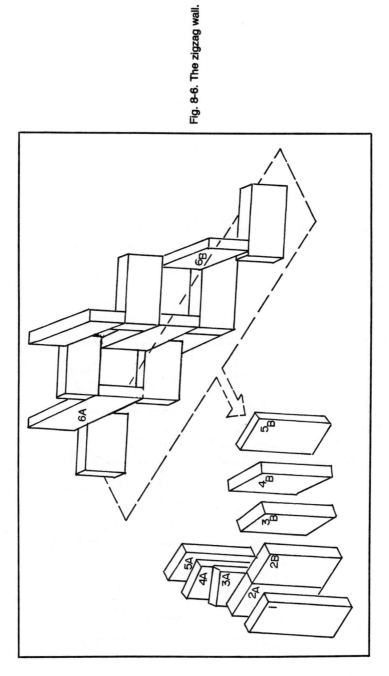

Fig. 8-6. The zigzag wall.

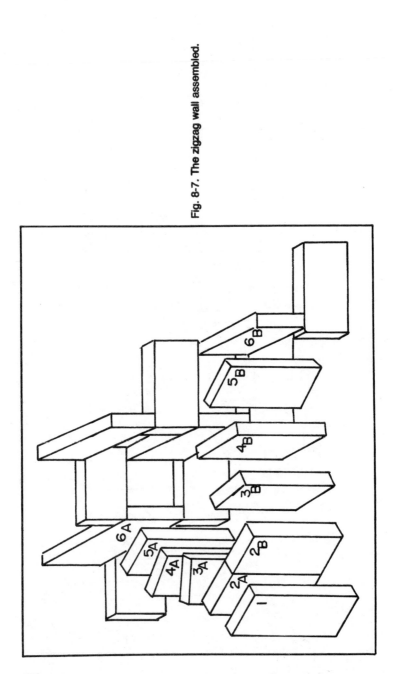

Fig. 8-7. The zigzag wall assembled.

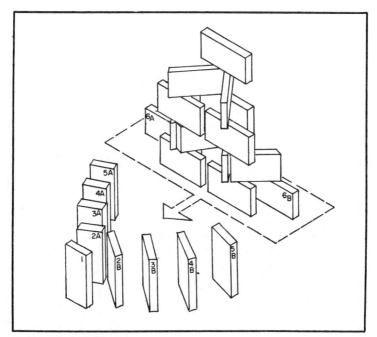

Fig. 8-8. The collapsible wall.

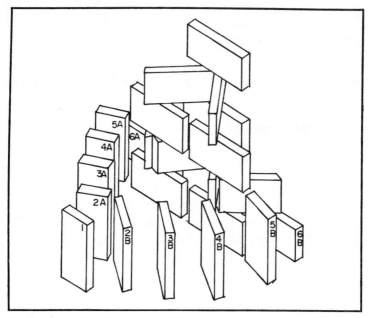

Fig. 8-9. The collapsible wall assembled.

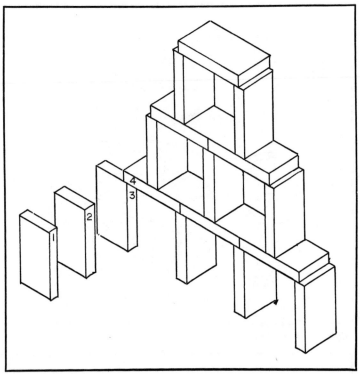

Fig. 8-10. The ultimate wall.

full of holes and the wall shown in Fig. 8-8 cannot be seen through. Any number of variations of these wall can be invented without much time or effort.

THE ULTIMATE WALL

Complexity: 2
POS: 5

This system is the best all-around wall (Fig. 8-10). This wall is very unstable. It can be set off from one end and the entire wall will fall. With a sufficient number of dominoes, this wall gives the highest and most dramatic fall of them all!

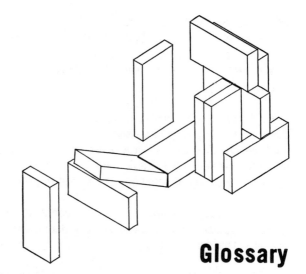

Glossary

backward—Dominoes falling right to left.
branch—A method for splitting a string of dominoes.

complexity rating—How difficult a trick is to assemble. A rating of 1 means the trick is very simple. A rating of 5 means the trick is very difficult.

D—The depth of one domino. It is always the smallest dimension of a domino.
domino dropper—A domino that is flipped onto another domino as a trick is triggered.

face—Each domino has three surfaces called faces.
flicked domino—The domino set into motion to begin a trick.
forward—Dominoes falling left to right.

H—The height of one domino. The length of one domino.

lead dominoes—A short string of dominoes used to add power to the beginning of a trick.

movement arrow—Used to indicate the direction a domino or dominoes will fall.

POS—*See* probability of success.

probability of success—Indicates how often a trick will work. A rating of 1 means there is very little chance the trick will succeed. A rating of 5 means the trick will work almost every time.

slide domino—*See* flicked domino.

surface A—The ends of a domino.

surface B—The front or back of a domino.

surface C—The sides of a domino.

system—A group of dominoes assembled to produce a trick.

T—A technique for splitting a string of dominoes at 90 degrees.

table—The base of a trick formed with dominoes.

target—The domino or dominoes that trigger a trick.

W—The width of one domino is equal to one-half the height of a domino.

Y—*See* branch.

Index

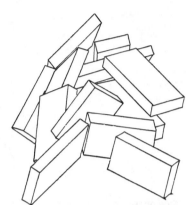

Index

Edited by Steven Bolt